ADVENTURES IN ANIMATION

HOW I LEARNED
WHO I LEARNED FROM
AND WHAT I DID WITH IT

RICHARD WILLIAMS

ADVENTURES IN ANIMATION

HOW I LEARNED
WHO I LEARNED FROM
AND WHAT I DID WITH IT

AND IMOGEN SUTTON

First published in 2024
by Faber & Faber Limited
The Bindery, 51 Hatton Garden
London EC1N 8HN

Typeset by Faber & Faber Limited
Printed in India

A CIP record for this book
is available from the British Library

ISBN 978–0–571–35720–8

FSC
www.fsc.org

MIX
Paper from
responsible sources
FSC® C016779

2 4 6 8 10 9 7 5 3 1

To our adventures, Moby Dick

CONTENTS

AUTHOR NOTE

As can be seen in the first twenty-two pages of the book, Dick intended to handwrite and lay out the pages of *Adventures in Animation* himself, but his work was cut short by illness and his subsequent death in 2019. I have developed the rest of the book using material Dick and I had been working on for many years, and this has been typeset and laid out using his early pages as our guide.

Imogen Sutton

FOREWORD
Actually, FOUR WORDS:
I • AM • VERY • LUCKY

WHEN WE WERE PUTTING TOGETHER "The Animator's Survival Kit" BOOK, I LOVED WORKING ON A BIG SECTION ABOUT the GREAT ANIMATORS I WAS SO FORTUNATE TO HAVE KNOWN, WORKED WITH and/or LEARNED FROM.

BUT IMOGEN (MO) MY WIFE and COLLABORATOR and WALTER DONOHUE (our editor at Faber) BOTH AGREED, "THAT ISN'T FOR THIS BOOK. THAT'S FOR ANOTHER BOOK."

AND THIS IS THAT BOOK.

I WAS IN the RIGHT PLACE AT the RIGHT TIME TO GET HELP FROM SO MANY UNUSUALLY TALENTED PEOPLE. I'M ALWAYS TELLING STORIES TO YOUNG ARTISTS ABOUT THEM and MY EXPERIENCES IN the MEDIUM. THEY KEEP SAYING, "WE WANT TO KNOW THIS STUFF. YOU'VE GOT TO WRITE IT DOWN."

I THOUGHT IF I PUT IN SPECIFIC THINGS I LEARNED FROM EACH ONE OF THEM, IT COULD BE USEFUL TO ANIMATORS and ARTISTS.

I'M WRITING THIS AT the FRIGHTENING AGE OF 86 and HAVE WORKED IN ANIMATION FOR 70 YEARS!

MO and I HAVE BEEN TOGETHER and WORKED TOGETHER FOR 35 YEARS – HALF of THAT TIME. MO JOINS IN BY NARRATING PARTS OF the BOOK WITH OUR VITAL EXPERIENCES IN and OUT OF the HOLLYWOOD MILL– the UPS and DOWNS, SUCCESSES TURNED INTO FAILURES, FAILURES TURNED INTO SUCCESSES, DEFEATS, TRIUMPHS and WONDERS ALONG the WAY.

I'VE ALWAYS BEEN TRYING TO EXTEND the MEDIUM –TO PUSH IT FURTHER IN DIFFERENT DIRECTIONS – BUT AT the SAME TIME I HAD TO

1

MASTER the TRADITIONAL ASPECTS OF the CRAFT AT EVERY LEVEL.

MO SAYS," THERE'S ONE THING THAT YOU CAN SAY ABOUT DICK— HE'S A LEARNER."

I WAS BORN INTO A TALENTED FAMILY IN TORONTO, the RICHEST CITY IN A RICH COUNTRY (CANADA) IN the MIDDLE OF the GREAT DEPRESSION, YET WAS ABLE EARLY ON TO EARN ENOUGH CASH TO TRAVEL WIDELY and DEVELOP WHATEVER NATURAL ABILITY I HAD AS SOME SORT OF ARTIST.

I'VE PUT IN 'ASSORTED SNAPSHOTS' UP TO AGE 20 WHEN MY CHARACTER IS PRETTY MUCH FORMED – CALL IT the "CHARACTER DEVELOPMENT" DEPARTMENT.

AFTER THAT I'M UNLEASHED INTO WHAT THEY CALL the "ADULT WORLD". (Well, at least the realities of the fully professional world.)

FROM THEN ON THIS BECOMES A

"GRAPH - O - GRAPHY"

A KIND OF PICTURE BOOK OF MY PROFESSIONAL LIFE.

IT'S MY STORY FROM AGE 2 TILL 86 and STILL GOING: HOW I WENT FROM ANIMATING SYMBOLIC GRAPHIC CHARACTERS – CARTOONS THAT CONVEYED IDEAS – THROUGH DOING EVERY KIND OF COMMERCIAL ANIMATION, SHORTS, TELEVISION and FEATURE FILMS.

IT'S WHAT I LEARNED ALONG the WAY – WHO I LEARNED IT FROM (INCLUDING SOME OF the BEST IN the WORLD) TO EVENTUALLY GAIN the ARTISTIC MUSCLE TO ARRIVE AT MY GOAL :

TO BE ABLE TO ANIMATE ANYTHING I CAN THINK OF – and MAKE IT CONVINCING.

STARTING OUT

MY FIRST TEACHER – MY GRANDAD,
CHARLIE BELL, BY MY UNCLE HARRY.

I SPENT the FIRST YEARS OF MY LIFE PLAYING WITH the WOOD, OFF-CUTS and SHAVINGS ON the FLOOR OF MY GRANDFATHER'S CARPENTRY SHOP.

I'VE BEEN TRYING TO RECREATE THAT SCENE IN SOME FORM OR ANOTHER FOR the REST OF MY LIFE – the SMELL OF the WOOD, the TOOLS, the ORGANISED WORLD OF A WORKSHOP and the THRILL OF MAKING THINGS.

THROUGH the BACK ALLEY, PLANKS OF LUMBER WOULD COME IN and FINISHED CHAIRS, CUPBOARDS and TABLES WOULD GO OUT.

IT SEEMED TO ME TO BE A WORLD OF MAGIC and I SENSED THAT MY GRANDAD WAS IN CONTROL OF EVERYTHING.

I'M IN FRONT OF GRANDAD'S WORKSHOP. IT WAS PAINTED GREEN and SO I ALWAYS HAVE PAINTED MY STUDIOS GREEN.

ONE THING I CLEARLY REMEMBER WAS WHEN I LOOKED UP FROM the WORKSHOP FLOOR, MANY OF the MEN WHO BROUGHT the WOOD and TOOK FINISHED THINGS AWAY DIDN'T SPEAK LIKE GRANDAD DID.

I DIDN'T KNOW WHAT the WORDS WERE BUT I KNEW THEY WERE UGLY — NOT LIKE GRANDAD'S WORDS. (There was a lot of racism around.)

GRANDAD THOUGHT I WAS REALLY SOMETHING, BECAUSE BEFORE I COULD WALK I WOULD GRAB A SCREWDRIVER and CRAWL TO the MAIN HOUSE and UNSCREW ALL the LOWER KITCHEN CUPBOARDS and TAKE ALL the DOORS OFF.

HE INDULGED and ENCOURAGED ME WHATEVER I DID.

BEING A TOUGH-MINDED YORKSHIREMAN, HE HAD HIS OWN IDEAS HOW EVERYTHING SHOULD BE and HE'D DO EVERYTHING HIS WAY.

WHEN HIS CHILDREN ASKED HIM TO BUILD A LARGE TABLE, HE'D BUILD THEM A SMALLER ONE. "WHY SHOULD YOU NEED SUCH A LARGE TABLE?"

HE WOULD BE THIS WAY WITH EVERYBODY. EXCEPT ME!

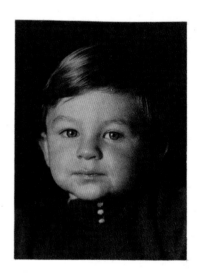

I REMEMBER GETTING HIM TO ALTER and REMAKE PARTS OF BOATS and TRAINS TO MY EXACT SPECIFICATIONS WHEN I COULD BARELY SPEAK.

AND HE DID IT EXACTLY AS I WANTED IT OVER and OVER UNTIL IT WAS "RIGHT". HE DID IT UNTIL I LEFT CANADA WHEN I WAS 20. HE MADE ME DESKS, RABBIT HUTCHES, EVERYTHING.

WHEN I DID PROFESSIONAL PUPPET SHOWS IN MY TEENS, HE DESIGNED and MADE A LARGE FOLD-UP STAGE TO FIT PERFECTLY INTO the SMALL MORRIS MINOR CONVERTIBLE CAR BOUGHT FROM MY COMMERCIAL ART EARNINGS.

HE CERTAINLY UNLEASHED the DEMANDING FILM DIRECTOR IN ME.

WHEN I WAS ABOUT 28, I WROTE HIM A THANK-YOU LETTER FOR EVERYTHING HE HELPED ME TO BE ABLE TO DO.

HE WAS 80, RECEIVED the LETTER, HAD IT ON HIM WHEN HE WAS WALKING HAND-IN-HAND WITH MY GRANDMOTHER WHEN HE JUST SLID SLOWLY TO the GROUND.

SOME FAMILY BACKGROUND:
CHARLIE BELL (born 1881) WAS DESCENDED FROM GENERATIONS OF ENGLISH CORDSWAINERS (makers of shoes) BUT HE COULDN'T STAND SHOES and BROKE the CHAIN BY BECOMING A CARPENTER.

HE EMIGRATED TO CANADA IN 1901 WHERE the STREETS WERE SAID TO BE PAVED WITH GOLD. THEY WEREN'T. AND THEY WEREN'T PAVED.

CHARLIE'S YOUNGER BROTHER, WILLIE, LEFT ENGLAND WITH HIM TO HELP HIM BUILD A SMALL HOUSE IN TORONTO. WHEN the GREAT WAR STARTED IN 1914, WILLIE WENT BACK TO ENGLAND TO ENLIST.

HE WAS KNOWN AS "LUCKY WILLIE" BECAUSE ALL the SOLDIERS IN the TRENCHES TRIED TO GET AS CLOSE AS POSSIBLE TO WILLIE. HE SEEMED TO HAVE A CHARMED LIFE AS BULLETS AVOIDED HIM — BUT NOT THAT CHARMED, BECAUSE HE WAS LEFT WITH SEVERE LUNG PROBLEMS FROM HAVING BEEN GASSED.

CHARLIE WAS LUCKY TOO. THERE WAS NO CONSCRIPTION IN CANADA.

ONCE IN the PROMISED LAND and BEING the HATED ENGLISH, CHARLIE and WILLIE WERE STONED BY TORONTO'S SCOTS-IRISH IMMIGRANTS AS THEY BATTLED TO BUILD the FOUNDATIONS OF A SMALL HOUSE.

CHARLIE'S FIANCÉ, EDITH BAINBRIDGE FOLLOWED, GOT OFF the BOAT at LAKE ONTARIO and THEY MARRIED ON the SPOT.

KAY BELL, MY MOTHER

MY MOTHER, KATHLEEN, WAS THEIR FIRST CHILD, FOLLOWED BY FIVE OTHERS: PEGGY (my godmother) and FOUR BROTHERS, NORMAN, HARRY, KEN and BILL.

MOM TOLD US THAT AS A LITTLE KID SHE WASN'T ALLOWED TO READ AT HOME. THEY WERE CRAFTSPEOPLE and THEY WEREN'T INTERESTED IN BOOKS. THEY DIDN'T SEE ANY PURPOSE IN IT.

SO MOM WOULD STOP AT the LIBRARY ON the WAY HOME TO READ FOR 15 MINUTES AT A TIME.

BEING the OLDEST OF SIX KIDS, SHE HAD TO HELP OUT WITH EVERYTHING and WHEN THEY DISCOVERED HER NATURAL TALENT FOR DRAWING WOULD BRING HOME MONEY, SHE LEFT SCHOOL AT 17 TO BECOME A COMMERCIAL ARTIST. SHE TOLD ME SHE WAS ASTONISHED WHEN SHE PICKED UP A PENCIL. "IT WAS LIKE MAGIC."

SHE TOLD ME THAT SHE and ANOTHER GIRL HAD TIED FOR A CROSS-CANADA PIANO and COMPOSITION SCHOLARSHIP, BUT SHE WASN'T ALLOWED TO CONTINUE.

THAT WAS PUT TO A STOP SO SHE COULD EARN MONEY FOR the FAMILY.

WHEN SHE ASKED WHY SHE and HER SISTER PEGGY HAD ONLY ONE NAME WHILE the FOUR BOYS EACH HAD TWO NAMES, HER DAD SAID, "GIRLS ONLY NEED ONE NAME."

MOM'S GOOD-LOOKING SISTER PEG (my godmother) WAS A SKILLED SEAMSTRESS WHO OFTEN FILLED IN AS SURROGATE MOTHER TO ME WHEN MOM WAS AWAY WORKING. SHE WAS ALWAYS VERY KIND TO ME.

THE ELDEST BROTHER WAS NORMAN, "the SLOW ONE", ACCORDING TO MOM,

NOT THAT SLOW! NORM SHONE IN HIS IMPORTANT WORK IN CHARGE OF 70 DRAFTSMEN AT DEHAVILLAND

MOM'S SISTER, PEGGY

AIRCRAFT, BUILDING the INNOVATIVE ALL-WOOD 'MOSQUITO' FIGHTER-BOMBER.

NORM LET ME HAVE SMALL REPLICAS OF IT TO PLAY WITH AS HE WORKED ON PLANS.

NORMAN

IT WAS CONSIDERED ONE OF CANADA'S GREAT CONTRIBUTIONS TO THE ALLIED WAR EFFORT.

THE NEXT BROTHER, HARRY, WAS A MULTI-TALENTED CRAFTSMAN ARTIST/DESIGNER WORKING AS A COMMERCIAL ARTIST.

ALTHOUGH HE WAS IN the ARMY IN the WAR, HE WAS A CONSCIENTIOUS OBJECTOR (you can imagine how many latrines he had to clean.) THAT MUST HAVE BEEN A TOUGH POSITION TO SUSTAIN AGAINST the WAR FEVER OF the TIMES, BUT HE DID.

MOM BOUGHT HER NEXT BROTHER, KEN, HIS FIRST

HARRY

CAMERA FROM HER ART EARNINGS and HE BECAME ONE OF the TOP PHOTOGRAPHERS IN CANADA.

KEN WAS A WAR PHOTOGRAPHER ON D-DAY ON the NORMANDY LANDINGS. HIS COLOUR SHOTS ARE the ONLY SURVIVING COLOUR PHOTOS OF the LANDINGS.

HE RECORDED the LIBERATION OF FRANCE, BELGIUM and the NETHERLANDS THROUGH TO the GERMAN SURRENDER.

HIS WAR EXPERIENCES LED HIM TO BECOME AN OFFICER COMMANDING OF the ROYAL REGIMENT OF CANADA and THEN AS the REGIMENT'S HONORARY LIEUTENANT-COLONEL.

KEN

The YOUNGEST BROTHER WAS BILL, WITH AN ENGINEERING OR MATHEMATICAL MIND WHO BECAME A SPITFIRE PILOT.

BILL

BILL WAS SO ADEPT AT FLYING, THEY KEPT HIM AS AN INSTRUCTOR FOR MOST OF the WAR.

"GEE," I SAID, "IT MUST BE GREAT FLYING SPITFIRES."

HE SAID, "SITTING UP THERE FOR THREE HOURS FREEZING YOUR ASS OFF?"

HIS FIRST TRAINEE, DOING HIS SOLO FLIGHT, DIDN'T PULL OUT OF HIS DIVE and WENT STRAIGHT INTO the GROUND. THIS HAUNTED BILL.

TOWARDS the END OF the WAR HE FLEW TYPHOON FIGHTER-BOMBERS TRAIN-BUSTING IN HOLLAND. HE GOT SHOT DOWN BUT SURVIVED.

"WAS HE HURT?" I ASKED HIS WAR PHOTOGRAPHER BROTHER, KEN.

KEN SAID, "NAW, BUT THAT WAS A HELL OF AN EXPENSIVE PIECE OF MACHINERY HE SMASHED UP."

AFTER the WAR, BILL BECAME A TOP EXECUTIVE IN the DUPONT CHEMICALS CORP. SADLY, WHAT HE REALLY WANTED TO DO WAS BE AN ARTIST.

MOM TOLD HIM (ACCURATELY) THAT HE WASN'T GOOD ENOUGH - THOUGH HE PAINTED EVERY CHANCE HE COULD GET ALL HIS LIFE - CHURCHES, etc. WITH EVERY BRICK IN PLACE.

THESE RELATIVES OF MINE WERE AN UNUSUALLY GIFTED GROUP OF SIBLINGS and CANADA CERTAINLY WAS the LAND OF OPPORTUNITY FOR THEM.

IN the FATHER DEPARTMENT: I DIDN'T HAVE ONE.

HE WAS GONE WHEN I WAS TWO and I CAN'T REMEMBER HIM AT ALL.

THINGS CHANGE...

I DON'T KNOW WHY BUT I SPENT MY 4TH YEAR WITH MOM IN A SPARE
ROOM AT MY AUNT PEGGY'S HOUSE AT the SUBURBAN EDGE OF the CITY.
NO WORKSHOP. NO GRANDAD. NO UNCLES. NOT MUCH MOM.

PEG HAD MARRIED WALTER, AN ADVERTISING SALESMAN and THEY
ALREADY HAD MY 2-YEAR-OLD COUSIN JOHN TO LOOK AFTER.

PEG WAS WORN OUT, WALTER WAS DIFFICULT and I WAS A NERVOUS WRECK.

MOM WAS OUT WORKING ALL HOURS and GRANDMA WOULD VISIT TO FILL IN-
SO MUCH SO THAT I THOUGHT I HAD 2 MOTHERS: MOM and BIGMOM.

MOM and BIGMOM WOULD COME and GO and I REMEMBER THROWING HEARTBROKEN FITS WHEN EITHER LEFT.

I WAS NEVER ABLE TO CALL BIGMOM GRANDMA, ONLY BIGMOM — EVEN WHEN I WENT TO SEE HER AS SHE WAS APPROACHING DEATH.

I DO HAVE A CLEAR MEMORY OF BEING UPSTAIRS IN the BATHROOM and HEARING A FURIOUS WALTER BELLOWING FROM BELOW, "HE'S JUST LIKE the REST OF HIS FAMILY!"

WHICH ONE? THE BELL FAMILY OR MY FATHER'S FAMILY? (of which I knew nothing.)

GROWING UP, I LEARNED THAT MY FATHER'S NAME WAS LESLIE LANE. HE ALSO WAS A COMMERCIAL ARTIST – A 'RETOUCHER' – TOUCHING UP PHOTOS – PUTTING the SHINE ON COKE BOTTLES, etc.

APPARENTLY HE WAS VERY CLEVER AT IT and ALTHOUGH IT WAS DURING the GREAT DEPRESSION, MOM TOLD ME HE EARNED LOTS and LOTS OF MONEY.

HE WAS FRONT MAN FOR A SMALL CO-OP STUDIO and MOM WAS the STAR ARTIST. SHE WAS A NATURAL FIGURE ARTIST SPECIALISING IN BABIES.

MY UNCLE HARRY TOLD ME THAT WHEN LES DELIVERED MOM'S ARTWORK TO the CLIENT, HE WOULD STOP OFF TO SIGN IT "LES LANE."

LES WAS ALSO A SERIAL WOMANISER and A SERIAL LIAR. MOM SAID, "IF HE EVER DID TELL the TRUTH, IT SOUNDED LIKE A LIE."

LES TOLD MOM THAT A MODEL THEY USED NEEDED MONEY AS SHE'D GOTTEN PREGNANT BY SOMEONE and SO THEY SHOULD HELP HER FINANCIALLY.

MOM LIKED HER and SO THEY PAID FOR the BIRTH etc.

IT TURNS OUT the LITTLE GIRL WAS BORN ALMOST the SAME DAY AS ME. MUCH LATER I REALISED I HAD A HALF-SISTER.

IT ALSO BECAME APPARENT THAT LES HAD BEEN EMBEZZLING the COMPANY'S MONEY.

KEN WILLIAMS (who was destined to become my stepfather) WORKED IN the STUDIO AS A SALESMAN, BEFRIENDED MY MOM and HELPED SET UP the COURT CASE and DIVORCE.

LES LEFT the COUNTRY FOR the USA.

The BIG JUMP

THE 5TH YEAR OF MY EXISTENCE EVERYTHING CHANGED.

MOM and KEN WILLIAMS MARRIED and WE MOVED TO A MOCK TUDOR HOUSE OUT BY TORONTO'S CITY LIMITS, SANDWICHED BETWEEN A HUGE WORKING CLASS AREA ON ONE SIDE and WEALTHY MANSIONS ON the OTHER, GOLF COURSE, HILLS and RAVEENS at the END OF the ROAD.

WITH MOM and KEN BRINGING IN TWO INCOMES, THEY MADE A MAJOR JUMP FROM WORKING CLASS TO PUSHING UPPER MIDDLE.

AND WHAT PAID FOR IT?

ADVERTISING.

IT'S NO SURPRISE THAT THEY ALWAYS HAD A PRO ADVERTISING BIAS. WHAT OTHER WAY COULD THEY HAVE DONE IT?

THEY BOTH WORKED LIKE MAD, MOM BOTH AT HOME and AWAY.

I HAD A MARVELLOUS NANNY – A BIG BLACK WOMAN CALLED BEULA, WHO I LOVED TO PIECES.

THERE WAS A LOT OF ACTIVITY IN THIS NEW SITUATION.

I REMEMBER LYING IN the BACK OF the CAR AS WE SPED AROUND TO DIFFERENT PLACES.

THERE WASN'T A LOT OF PHYSICAL HUGGING, BUT MOM and I HAD A LIFETIME OF DEEP CONNECTION and TRUST.

SHE PUT ME IN the LOCAL KINDERGARTEN and I VAGUELY REMEMBER GETTING A LOT OF ATTENTION FOR PAINTING A BIG PICTURE OF the KING and QUEEN, WHICH CAUSED QUITE A FUSS.

SOMEHOW I KNEW I WAS AN ARTIST AT AGE 2 – I JUST SEEMED TO KNOW IT.

ONE DAY KEN TOOK ME INTO the LARGE BACK YARD and SAID, "I DON'T WANT YOU TO CALL ME KEN ANY MORE, BECAUSE NOW I'M YOUR FATHER. CALL ME DAD. I'M YOUR DAD NOW."

WHAT ELSE COULD I SAY? "YES, DAD."

KEN TOOK FATHERHOOD SERIOUSLY.

TO BOND WITH ME, HE TOOK ME TO ALL SORTS OF FASCINATING EVENTS WHICH MADE STRONG IMPRESSIONS ON ME THAT WOULD PAY OFF FOR the REST OF MY LIFE.

I'D BEEN 4 WHEN I WAS TAKEN TO the RINGLING BROTHERS 3 RING CIRCUS and I WENT CRAZY ABOUT the ELEPHANTS.

WHEN THEY WERE LEAVING THERE WAS A MOMENTARY SILENCE.

MY PIERCING FALSETTO SHOT THROUGH the AIR OF the ENTIRE STADIUM, "OOOOOOOO HELEPHAAAAAAANTSCOMMMBAAAAAAACK!"

THE NEXT YEAR DAD and I HAD RINGSIDE SEATS AT the SAME CIRCUS.

THE STAR ACT WAS A WOMAN WAY UP AT the TOP OF the STADIUM WHO WOULD LEAP FROM ONE SWING TO ANOTHER WHICH WAS SENT IN the AIR TOWARDS HER TO LEAP INTO SPACE and CATCH. AND WITHOUT A NET.

WHEN SHE WAS PREPARING FOR the LEAP, I STARTED FREAKING OUT.

"DAD! YOU'VE GOT TO STOP THIS! STOP IT NOW! SHE'S GOING TO FALL!"

HE TRIED TO SHUSH ME. "CALM DOWN. DON'T WORRY. SHE DOES THIS EVERY DAY-TWICE A DAY. SHE NEVER FALLS."

"NO! I TELL YOU! SHE'S GOING TO FALL! YOU MUST STOP THEM!"

"NO! SIT DOWN! SHE WON'T FALL!"

SHE FELL.

ALL the WAY DOWN TOWARDS US IN A KIND OF RUNNING POSITION - HITTING the GROUND RIGHT IN FRONT OF US.

THEY ZIPPED HER OUT and the SHOW WENT ON. THE PAPERS SAID SHE SOMEHOW SURVIVED, BUT WAS ALL BROKEN UP FOR LIFE.

DAD HAD AN INTEREST IN MAGIC and TOOK ME TO the ROYAL ALEXANDRA THEATRE TO SEE "BLACKSTONE - the WORLD'S GREATEST MAGICIAN."

THE HOUSE WAS PACKED, BUT WE WERE SITTING IN the FRONT ROW and AT A CERTAIN POINT BLACKSTONE ASKED FOR A CHILD VOLUNTEER.

SOMEHOW I FOUND MYSELF CENTRE STAGE WITH the GREAT MAGICIAN IN FRONT OF 2000 PEOPLE. SEVERAL AMAZING THINGS HAPPENED, CULMINATING WITH ME HOLDING A LOAF OF BREAD WHICH I PULLED APART TO REVEAL A GREY BUNNY INSIDE.   BOY, DID I LIKE THAT!

MY GRANDAD MADE ME A FINE RABBIT HUTCH and I LEFT FOR 2 WEEKS TO the YMCA SUMMER CAMP UP NORTH IN the MUSKOKA LAKES.

WHEN I RETURNED HOME, the HUTCH WAS THERE BUT MY RABBIT WAS GONE. THE NIGHT BEFORE I LEFT I HAD MISTAKEN CREAM FOR MILK and the POOR THING COULDN'T DIGEST IT and DIED.

DAD ALSO TOOK ME TO CRAZY WRESTLING MATCHES: WHIPPER BILLY WATSON (with blood flying) and SPIKE JONES and HIS CITY SLICKERS COMIC ORCHESTRA and OLSEN and JOHNSON'S HILARIOUS REVIEW, "HELZAPOPPIN" -- ALL THIS STUFF OUT OF the ORDINARY.

THERE WAS A LITTLE THEATRE IN TORONTO WHERE the LAST DAYS OF VAUDEVILLE STILL PLAYED OUT.

WE SAW ALL the FAMOUS OLD PERFORMERS ON THEIR LAST LEGS and ALL the GREAT TIMING and COMIC INVENTION (so important in animation) MADE LASTING IMPRESSIONS ON ME.

THEY ALWAYS HAD A SMALL ORCHESTRA and DAD LATER TOLD ME THAT WHENEVER the MUSIC WAS "BUSY" WITH SEPARATE LINEAR LINES ALL GOING AT ONCE (and fitting together as in Dixieland jazz or classical fugues) I WOULD JUMP UP and DOWN IN MY SEAT.

MAGIC

WALT DISNEY'S FIRST FEATURE-LENGTH CARTOON,"SNOW WHITE and the SEVEN DWARFS"HAD JUST BEEN FINISHED (1938) and OPENED IN CANADA AT the ROYAL ALEXANDRA THEATRE IN TORONTO.

MOM and DAD TOOK ME the FIRST WEEK. I THINK IT WAS the FIRST FILM I SAW. BOOM! THE WORLD OF the IMAGINATION MADE MANIFEST!

THERE'D BEEN NOTHING LIKE IT EVER BEFORE. IT'S HARD TO IMAGINE TODAY the IMPACT THIS FILM HAD AT THAT TIME.

I CAN'T DESCRIBE the IMPACT IT HAD ON ME. I WAS TRANSPORTED INTO ANOTHER DIMENSION - ANOTHER REALM. MY ENTRY INTO the WORLD OF the IMAGINATION OPENED WIDE.

DRAWINGS THAT WALKED and TALKED! AND LIVED IN A WORLD OF PAINTINGS - and SOMEHOW WITH MUSIC!

I'D SEEN MOM MAKING SOME DRAWINGS OF the DWARFS and PRINCESS AT HOME, SO I KNEW THAT the ENTIRE THING WAS MADE BY PEOPLE WITH PENCILS IN THEIR HANDS.

WHEN MY MOM WAS DYING, I SAID SOMETHING TO HER LIKE," DO YOU THINK I'VE BEEN DRIVEN TO HAVE the CAREER THAT YOU COULD OF HAD, OR SHOULD HAVE HAD?"

"NONSENSE!" SHE SNAPPED."YOU WERE FIVE WHEN YOU SAW `SNOW WHITE' and YOU WERE NEVER the SAME AGAIN!"

IT'S TRUE. IT OPENED MY MIND WIDE.

LITTLE DID I KNOW THAT I WOULD EVENTUALLY MEET, BECOME FRIENDS WITH and/or LEARN FROM SEVERAL OF the MAIN ARTISTS WHO MADE the GREAT FILM: DICK HUEMER, ART BABBITT, GRIM NATWICK, FRANK THOMAS, WARD KIMBALL, OLLIE JOHNSTON and MILT KAHL.

A SHORT WHILE LATER I WAS TAKEN TO the NEXT BIG MOVIE HIT,"THE WIZARD OF OZ."

EVERYBODY LOVED IT. I DIDN'T.

I WAS TERRIBLY DISAPPOINTED. I DIDN'T LIKE IT BECAUSE IT WAS ABOUT "REAL" PEOPLE.

THE GIRL IN IT COULD HAVE BEEN the GIRL ACROSS the STREET.

THEY'D JUST PHOTOGRAPHED REAL ACTORS and SO THEY STAYED IN the SAME DIMENSION I WAS LIVING IN.

THIS WASN'T DRAWN BY HAND. THIS WASN'T MAGIC CREATED FROM NOTHING — THIS WAS JUST TAKING PICTURES OF PEOPLE ALL DRESSED UP and RUNNING AROUND.

SNOW WHITE and the DWARFS WERE STIMULATING BECAUSE THEY WERE CREATED BY ARTISTS. THEY DIDN'T LOOK LIKE REAL LITTLE PEOPLE. THEY WERE INVENTED! THEY WERE FUNNY and CHARMING.

IT WAS BECAUSE SNOW WHITE WASN'T REAL THAT IT HAD CREATED REALITY.

THE CONTRADICTION IS THAT I COULD BELIEVE THEM BEING MUCH MORE REAL, BECAUSE THEY WEREN'T REAL.

SOMEHOW HERE IS the DEFINITION OF ART: OUR WILLING SUSPENSION OF DISBELIEF.

I'M SOUNDING LIKE A FILM THEORIST HERE — BUT SOMEHOW MY TINY BRAIN AT the TIME FIGURED IT OUT OR JUST "FELT" IT.

THE THING IS: IT'S NOT REALISM — IT'S BELIEVABILITY.

18

MOM'S WORK

AS I GREW UP I SAW MOM CONSTANTLY DRAWING. AT FIRST I THOUGHT THAT'S WHAT ALL MOTHERS DID.

MY MOTHER HAD A REMARKABLE TALENT WHICH WAS NEVER PROPERLY FED, WATERED and ENCOURAGED TO BLOSSOM, SO SHE NEVER REACHED HER POTENTIAL.

IN THOSE DAYS IT WAS MUCH HARDER FOR AN INTELLIGENT, TALENTED WOMAN WHOSE PLACE WAS CONSIDERED TO BE IN the HOME.

SHE WAS A MARVELLOUS PERSON, ALWAYS ENCOURAGING TO ME, BUT WITH SHARP CRITICAL SENSE.

SOMEHOW OR OTHER SHE ENDED UP DOING LESS and LESS WORK, BUT INSTEAD OF WOMEN and CHILDREN, SHE WAS DOING DISNEY TOY BOXES and SHOES FOR CATALOGUES. SHE WOULD LET ME DRAW, PAINT and FILL IN LITTLE CORNERS OF HER WORK.

THIS IS the SORT OF WORK SHE DID FOR HERSELF IN HER LATE TEENS...

...and THIS IS WHAT SHE DID FOR A LIVING.

THIS REMAINS UNFINISHED — RATHER AS SHE WAS.

LIFE AT THE 'Y'

Meanwhile, the humdrum emptiness of the suburban world of Golfdale Road was very different from the interactions of the close-up family I'd been used to, and I was finding it difficult to adjust. Also, for some reason, my wonderful nanny had vanished.

Mom said I was becoming 'a sissy', afraid to leave the house, even though there were kids on the same street to play with. Her solution was brilliant. She sent me to the YMCA in the centre of the city. I had to take a bus and streetcar to get there and back on a Saturday. I was 5 or 6 years old.

One of the first things I did at the 'Y' was to fall off a parallel bar and dislocate my shoulder. The 'Y' guys took me to the General Hospital (where I'd been born) and I experienced my first run-in with bureaucracy. Dislocations can be very painful. This one certainly was and I spent hours in great pain, lying on a stretcher with my upper arm bone sticking way out (under the skin), trying to convince the staff that my parents could pay.

Eventually they contacted them, filled out some forms and, in a couple of minutes, popped the bone back in place.

There were three great things about the YMCA. The first thing was the swimming pool and Charlie Tinsley the swimming coach, a real tough character. I took to swimming immediately and later joined the team, becoming a competitive swimmer.

The second thing was that on Saturday afternoons after the gym and swim they ran old movies on a 16 mm film projector: Buster Keaton, Charlie Chaplin, the Keystone Kops and cartoons. I used to make notes as I watched – writing the names of the animators – then do a page analysis at home. I remember getting them to stop the projector frame by frame so I could trace the projected cartoon images on pieces of paper against the wall.

Gradually, I could tell who did what. One animator whose work I loved was Ken Harris – in the Warner Bros. shorts. I could spot his work because he drew in little square bits – he drew movements that were sparser and funnier than most. Stay tuned to discover the impact Ken made on me.

The third great thing was that a couple of blocks around the corner from the YMCA there was an all-cartoon cinema which ran all the wonderful cartoons of the day: Bugs Bunny, Donald Duck, Porky Pig, Goofy, Daffy Duck, Woody Woodpecker, Droopy, Wile E. Coyote and the Roadrunner, all of them. I haunted that cinema every Saturday for years.

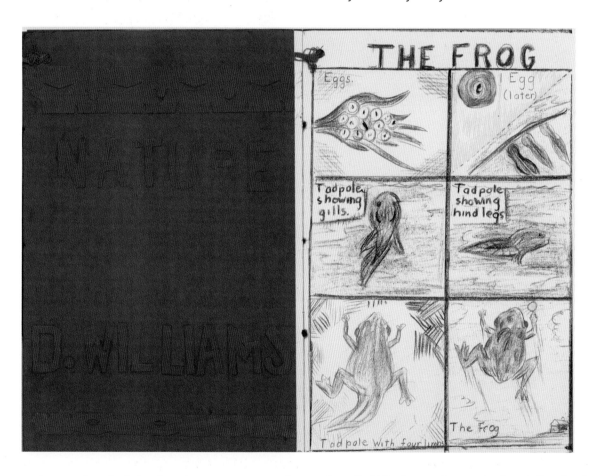

I was already into drawing movement at age 6 or 7. What surprises me about the final panel of this drawing, with the frog leaping, is that it has speed lines.

Quite often Dad would drive from Toronto along Lake Ontario to Niagara Falls, cross over into the USA and shop in Buffalo, New York. In those days there was no hassle crossing the border; we just seemed to drive across the bridge and we were in the States.

I recall we were walking along the streets in Buffalo and I was going along the curbside of the dirty sidewalk and gutter, strewn with cigar butts, chewing gum, wrappers and bottle caps.

I thought, Canada is so clean – and this is *very* dirty . . . long pause . . . but much more interesting!

Around the same time, for who knows what reason, my parents bought me a little tailor-made three-piece suit. When it was finished I got to see myself in multiple mirrors from all angles at once.

I said to Mom, 'You're very good-looking – most of our family are good-looking. You once told me that my biological father had movie-actor-like animal magnetism – what's it with how I look? How come I look like this?'

She said, 'Well, you came out part clown.'

I told Mom, 'I'm very disappointed.'

Exactly at that time, American comic books began to appear in Canada, and I was able to buy the very first editions of *Captain Marvel*, *Mandrake the Magician*, *The Human Torch*, *Namor the Sub-Mariner*, *Plastic Man*, and, most importantly, *Superman*, *Batman and Robin*, *Looney Tunes* and *Merrie Melodies* – all wild stuff to feed the imagination.

These comics were initially not allowed in Canada, presumably for fear of corrupting the minds of Canadian youth. But the authorities relented three or four years later and allowed them in. Of course, all the 'cultural' stuff spilled over the border from the USA. Nearly all the movies, magazines, books, radio programmes.

At the same time I was having the great Canadian outdoor experiences: YMCA summer camp, canoeing, portaging, crafts, swimming in a volcanic lake that was clear as a glass of water.

FASCINATION WITH MOVEMENT

There was an empty lot across the road from our house where we could play. I loved playing baseball but Mom told me later that I would always leave the game for short periods to run into the house because I just had to draw for a bit, then back out to the game.

Mom teased me that I was always drawing 'a running boy' (obviously influenced by Batman and Robin). A fascination with movement.

My pictures were always trying to move. In school, I was drawing as much as possible. We had a Grade 6 teacher, Miss Farrier, who was really nice-looking, wore lemon-yellow sweaters

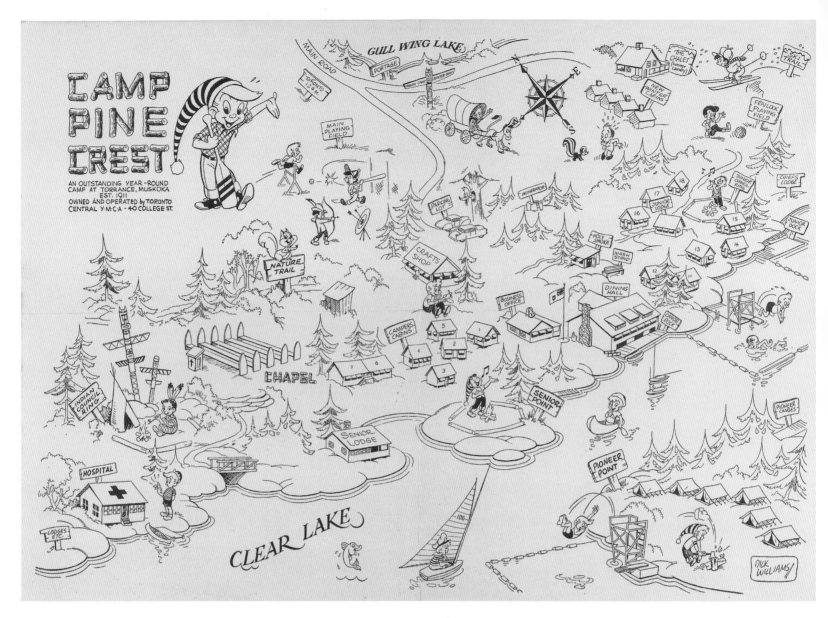

EVERY SUMMER I WENT NORTH TO the YMCA'S CAMP PINE CREST. I WAS
PRETTY MUCH AT HOME WITH the PLACE, AS YOU CAN TELL FROM MY MAP.
LOTS OF SWIMMING IN the VOLCANIC LAKE WHICH WAS CLEAR AS A GLASS
OF WATER. THEY STILL USE MY MAP AS POSTCARDS - (BUT WITHOUT MY NAME.)

and encouraged me to draw. Her boyfriend was a fighter pilot on service in England. She was
kind and we liked each other.

Here's my report card. Good start.

An honour pupil
(I should like to see Dick more prompt in obeying commands)
Excellent work!
Excellent indeed!
Very satisfactory indeed!

My dad, Ken, had flat feet so he'd been excused from the Army and continued as normal.

There was an interschool competition to create heroic war posters featuring soldiers, pilots, sailors, tanks, planes and ships. For three years I won it for the school. Then the fourth year I didn't win. I thought I'd done a really good entry and I asked the principal what had happened.

'You were disqualified – they said a child couldn't have done it.'

I'd absorbed some of Mom's commercial art facility by then. She'd always let me do little corners and bits of jobs on which she was working.

Here's my Grade 6 assessment (straight As). My teacher was Sandy McLellan. (She features in my *Survival Kit* book in the lip sync dialogue section.) She was enthusiastic and let some of us create comic books along with our other work.

V. satisfactory pupil
Excellent work
Good progress
Works well
Intelligent grasp

DARKENING CLOUDS

Grade 7 was next and brought the first darkening clouds. Kids said, 'You'll be lucky now, Dick, because Mr Martin loves art.' I didn't like Mr Martin, who was arty, but also pretentious and prissy. He wore a sort of cape. We didn't get on.

On one occasion he stamped me down to the principal, who pulled my pants down and lashed me with the belt strap. I had absolutely no idea why. This didn't help my concentration and my marks really started to slip from this point on. I was beginning to question authority:

Good marks but Dick does not co-operate
Mathematics, lower
Daydreams

'Daydreams' became a regular item on my report card with resultant trouble at home. 'You come from above-average parents and we expect above average marks.'

(That's true, but we weren't too sure about my biological father, were we?)

We had a tiny woodworking teacher, Mr Pomeroy, who terrified nearly everybody, but I got on with him somehow, partly because of my love of wood (it's alive!). He was very proud that one of his previous students had done the beautiful design and lettering for the main title of Disney's *Snow White* film.

Old Pomeroy was always in conflict with everybody – except me.

One morning I was early at school and was walking down the hall past his workshop. He had a large room with huge glass windows down two sides.

Every single window and every pane of glass was smashed.

He was alone, huddled over his desk in his workshop sobbing uncontrollably. I unexpectedly saw and felt the human side of an authoritarian.

At the same time, I was starting to become quite a good mimic and was drawing caricatures of the teachers in my books. I realised early on that satire and caricature are both an attack on and defence against the powerful by the powerless.

The totally humourless Mr Ankerman and the Grade 8 class photo. We must be 12-year-olds. I don't know why I'm at the front. Probably so Mr Ankerman could keep an eye on me and rebellious Michael Geary (front right). Mike was always in trouble. Note his body language. Weeks after this photo was taken, he got drunk, got into his dad's car, took off, drove into a tree and killed himself. My clever little half-smile and my tiny Bugs Bunny seem to me like I just wanted to get on with what I was doing. The drawing of a knight on a white horse, way at the back right, is mine.

GETTING TOUGH

When I was 12, my little brother Tony was born. He was to become far from little and also the brilliant lawyer our dad had always wanted to be.

When asked why he chose to be a prosecuting attorney, Tony said, 'Somebody has to protect the victims.' He has a lot of our mom in him.

For a while he was the youngest Queen's Counsel in Ontario.

He's always been a great friend to me. He's also a pack rat, and it's because he kept so much memorabilia of his older brother's experiences that we've been able to flesh out a lot of this book with relevant material.

The brothers as children and as older men

With Tony's arrival in the world I was no longer the centre of parental attention and I had a sudden burst of independence. Later on, my mom told my eldest son Alex, 'One day Dick suddenly got tough.'

Ted, a kid across the road, same age as me, was built stronger and a natural athlete. I was very skinny, had broken a couple of wrist bones, and he and his mom called me 'brittle bones'. For seven years Ted had given me a hard time, pushing me around. Now I decided to fight back.

I started a strategic psychological war against him with other kids, which ended up with me chasing him all the way home from school several days running until he stopped. We then had a big fight which ended in a draw. I never had any more trouble from Ted from then on and we were friendly. He ended up as a professional golfer.

The point is that from the age of 12 I started to travel around with more resilience and confidence, and an increased questioning of authority.

HIGH SCHOOL

Aged 13, I was off to high school, but not to the regular high school with my friends on the street. I was sent to a 'vocational' school mostly specialising in subjects to encourage students into engineering. They also had a full-on art course but my folks didn't want me to do that.

I was put in the engineering-centred department, with metal-lathe shop work and light carpentry, topped off by a double load of mathematics and physics. No art. Strange that I was not to flourish . . .

Years later I asked Mom, 'How come you sent me there?' She said, 'They lied to us.'

Just before I wrote this, my old friend Martin Hunter, who used to live across the street, phoned me up from Canada. (Martin became an actor, author and playwright, and we've always had much in common.)

Martin said, 'This is probably the last conversation we will ever have.' (It was. He died two days later.)

During our talk I said, 'I never could figure out why you went to the normal high school and I was sent to the vocational one.'

Martin said, 'Oh, that's because our parents got together and sent you, me and Ted to different schools to break us up as we were becoming too much trouble.'

This was in 1945. The war was over and a period of great prosperity and optimism began, especially in North America. All sorts of old and new movies poured out, and there was television.

At first, TV was rarely in people's homes. On Wednesday nights Martin and I would trudge up through the heavy winter snows to an appliance store on Yonge Street to stare through the window of the closed shop and watch the top TV show of the day – which from 1948 was the Milton Berle Show. There was no sound, but we were hypnotised by the crazy visual gags and old vaudeville routines.

We also went to the cinema to see the old Marx Brothers films. I laughed so much at *Duck Soup*, I almost broke my nose on the seat in front.

Martin could be very funny; we were always horsing around trying out comic routines, stealing gags from the radio and films and writing stuff of our own. Richie Brown, my pal and puppet show partner (also an artist) would often join us – he was a gifted impressionist.

I was just about managing in my 'chosen' school as I tried to rise to the physics and maths challenges, but was increasingly feeling a fish out of water. Also, it didn't help to constantly pass by the smiling faces of the kids in the art department. As my marks and morale deteriorated, I unconsciously started to develop a 'You can't fire me, I quit' attitude.

My way of dealing with difficult situations and authority was to be the clown. I used to clown for defence and satirise for attack. Gradually, the clown side and the satire side combined and 'Ivan Yurpee and his Yangtze River boys' burst forth. (I was Yurpee, and he had this clown orchestra.)

I found that the Northern Vocational School auditorium was bookable for outside events and I started to organise anybody in school who wanted to perform in a comic revue. My friends were always the musicians and we started to work on tailor-made routines. We began small, practising after school and we ended up with Show #4 on a pretty big scale, with a packed audience.

Jack Dale, a very clever pianist (an early bebopper) wrote ingenious arrangements for the twenty-two-piece orchestra we created of students plus some outsiders, the latter much to the irritation of the music department. (I recently rediscovered some of Jack's scores for us and they were very professional!)

Everybody made their own costumes, Martin and I did most of the script, and we all pitched in wherever we could.

My uncle Harry was impressed with our performance #3 and volunteered to be a stager for #4. He made all kinds of props, including an exploding outhouse (toilet). So we had a cast of fifteen and an orchestra of twenty-two – thirty-seven people!

The school had to grudgingly put up with it all, because I cleverly talked the North Toronto YMCA into sponsoring the whole thing. While it was very wild, satiric and edgy, there was nothing you could call unwholesome.

We got some quite enthusiastic support from the teacher in the drama department, but my woodworking teacher, Mr Norris, was very disapproving and gave me a hard time. (He was an enthusiastic Gilbert and Sullivan performer.)

The head of the art department, L. A. C. Panton, RCA, OSA, would sometimes enter our school rehearsals to register silent disgust. He had an odd habit of bouncing up and down on his heels; he was very stiff in a tight suit and tie, shoes as shiny as glass. Could this guy really be an artist?

Meanwhile, my academic struggle continued, but I had an unlikely ally – Mr Crich. Victor Crich (pronounced KREYECH) taught us geography. He was also a bird photographer, who had Fellow of the Royal Photographic Society (FRPS) after his name, and sometimes had his photos of birds in the newspaper.

He was a tough-guy teacher and everybody was scared of him, but he and I had something in common – neither of us wanted to be there. He wanted to be out in the wild, photographing birds, and I wanted to be drawing.

One day in class, he caught me trying to animate a cycle of a bird walking with a large plume flashing around. To my surprise Mr Crich said, 'That's very interesting. Keep going.'

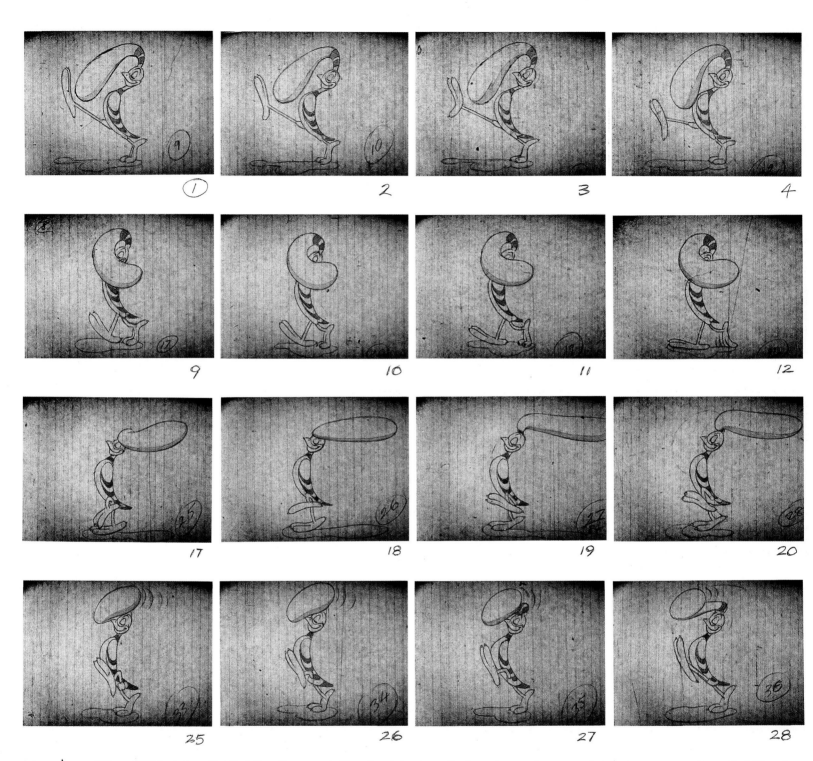

①	2	3	4
9	10	11	12
17	18	19	20
25	26	27	28

HERE'S A LITTLE MIRACLE OF RESTORATION FROM 70 YEARS AGO. I'D SAVED THESE BIRD DRAWINGS FROM AGE 15. PBS BROADCASTING IN AMERICA 50 YEARS AGO MADE AN HOUR DOCUMENTARY ON ME FOR A TELEVISION SERIES CALLED "the CREATIVE PERSON". (of course it was black+white)

WE SHOT THESE DRAWINGS I'D MADE ON A RULED YELLOW LEGAL PAD ON A TEST CAMERA. SHE WALKED! AND WAS PUT IN the FILM. I'VE SINCE LOST the DRAWINGS BUT DISCOVERED I HAD A COPY of the SHOW and TOOK IT TO MY PALS at AARDMAN ANIMATIONS, "CAN WE PRINT THIS ONTO SHEETS OF PAPER?"

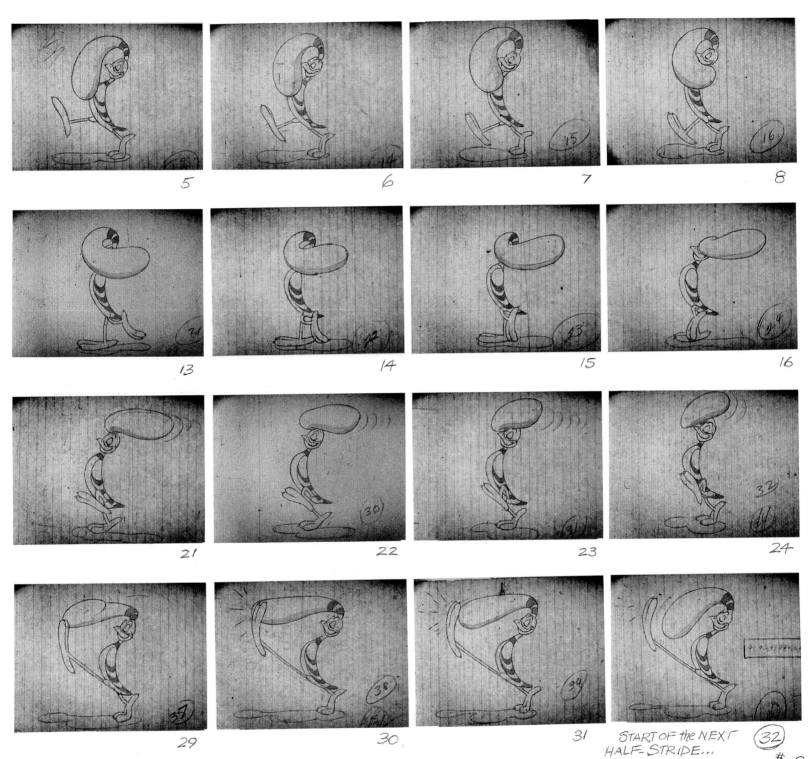

5   6   7   8

13   14   15   16

21   22   23   24

29   30.   31   START OF the NEXT HALF-STRIDE...   32

IT DISAPPEARED INTO the LAND of TECHNOLOGICAL TRIAL and ERROR, FINALLY PRODUCING A SEMI-VISIBLE BIRD ON GROTTY FILM. THEN the WONDERS of the COMPUTER ENHANCED the DRAWINGS and LIGHTENED the BACKGROUND. THEN I SHARPENED the DRAWINGS and SHE REAPPEARS OVER 70 YEARS LATER.

IGNORE MY ORIGINAL NUMBERS. WHY DID I START WITH #9? ONE THING I LEARNED IS TO THINK SIMPLY. ANIMATION IS COMPLEX ENOUGH WITHOUT ADDING COMPLICATIONS. I'M SURPRISED at the "SOPHISTICATED" MOVING HOLD of the FOOT #19 to #28 BEFORE IT SHOOTS OUT. I'D HESITATE TO DO THAT TODAY. AUDACITY of YOUTH.

33

After my first film *The Little Island* came out and I had an article in *Time* magazine, Mr Crich wrote me a letter saying how pleased he was to have spotted my ability and that he was thrilled I'd done so well.

When I visited home in Toronto I went to see him – he'd retired and was a full-time photographer. Happy at last.

Another ally was the assistant teacher to Panton. I only remember him as Percy – a nice guy. Percy spotted my work around the place and said, 'Good heavens, you draw better than anybody in the art graduating class. Why aren't you on the art course?'

I told him my parents thought it was best to be 'grounded'.

Percy said, 'Look, why don't you take the final exam in life drawing and I'll show your work to Mr Panton.'

I didn't know what that would do, but Percy let me in and I took the exam – drawing a seated woman posing in a yellow bathing suit.

Nothing happened for a couple of months, until I was told to go to the office of the head of art.

I knocked on the door and was told to sit on a chair facing L. A. C. Panton, RCA, OSA, who stood by a window, behind a desk at the other end of a narrow corridor of shelves packed with drawings and portfolios.

He said, 'I've seen your drawing', (taking his time) 'and I have to tell you . . . that you have no talent whatsoever.'

I said, 'Wasn't there *anything* you liked about it?'

Panton answered, 'Well, you could tell it was a woman, but that's about all.'

I said something like 'Oh dear, what shall I do?'

He said, 'You could make your living as a barber, or some job like that.'

That was it.

As my pockets were full of cash from my work (dog-food ads) in the newspapers and on twenty-four-sheet colour billboards, this didn't faze me at all; in fact, I found it kind of amusing.

Then I thought of all the impressive speeches educators make about their nurturing of young talent etc.

What if I hadn't already been confident of my abilities? That could have crushed an innocent 14- or 15-year-old kid.

I thought, 'Bugger you! I'll get you one day . . . .'

A SURPRISING THING HAPPENED WHEN I WAS 14 YEARS OLD.

MY ADVERTISING MAN FATHER KNEW the AD AGENCY PEOPLE WHO HAD the DR. BALLARD DOG and CAT FOOD ACCOUNT. THE ARTIST WHO DREW DISNEY-ISH DOGS and CATS FOR THEIR ADS HAD DIED. HE WAS CHARLES THORSON, A CANADIAN WHO HAD WORKED FOR DISNEY ON PRELIMINARY DESIGNS FOR the PRINCESS IN "SNOW WHITE." HE ALSO WORKED AT WARNER BROS. and HAD DESIGNED the FIRST MODEL SHEET OF BUGS BUNNY (WHICH WAS AT FIRST CALLED BUG'S BUNNY — AFTER ANIMATOR BUGS HARDAWAY, WHO THOUGHT HIM UP).

THORSON HAD RETURNED to CANADA and IN THOSE DAYS, FEW PEOPLE COULD DRAW THAT KIND OF STUFF CONVINCINGLY.

MY DAD SAID HE KNEW A YOUNG MAN WHO WAS EXPERT AT THAT SORT OF THING.

HE SHOWED THEM MY WORK and I WAS HIRED AT PROFESSIONAL RATES.

THEY NEVER KNEW IT WAS JUST A KID DOING the WORK and NEVER MET ME.
DAD WAS the GO-BETWEEN and I DREW ALL THEIR ADVERTISEMENTS UNTIL I WAS 18.
I WAS ABLE TO BUY A SMALL CAR AT 16!

Although these jobs began when I was in high school, they lasted during most of art school.

MUSIC

I had also wanted to learn the trumpet so I could play in the school orchestra, but after a music test, they said I didn't have enough ability to be given an instrument. They said I had no ear. I played by ear for many years before learning to read and write music, and becoming a lifelong semi-professional cornettist. At school I ended up struggling with a euphonium, but I could barely read music notation and I dropped out.

I bought an old cornet and a valve trombone and fiddled at home with both in a comic way, until I became serious and bought a good cornet with my dog-food advert earnings. Then start-ed my lifelong obsession with the cornet and later the trumpet (again) and the flugelhorn.

Something tremendous was happening. I heard music. I know I'd been hearing music all my life so far, but now I *heard* music! At 14, I heard everything at once!

I was friends with Jim Burke, a highly intel-ligent writer who lived at the 'Y' and looked after the locker rooms. Jim was a Beethoven de-votee and started me off with the late quartets and then the symphonies, alongside Gregorian chants, Monteverdi, Bach and Schubert.

At the same time, I saw the all-black music-al movie *Stormy Weather* and for the first time saw and heard Fats Waller with his seven-piece band (front line of trumpet, clarinet and trom-bone and rhythm section of piano, bass, guitar and drums). I jumped out of my skin. 'What is that? I want that!' They were playing Fats's composition 'Ain't Misbehavin'' – the same stuff, in the same instrumental line-up, that I would later spend my life playing. (It was 'fugal' music again but with 'rhythm'.)

Tep (Stephanie), my 12-year-old girlfriend, was musical, as was Bob, her pianist brother. They had all the jazz LP and 78 records of the original folk and blues bands, jug bands, gospel choirs, Lead Belly, Robert Johnson, Bessie Smith, 1920s jazz, Jelly Roll Morton, Dixieland, 1930s swing, Billie Holiday, 1940s bebop, cool jazz.

The early Louis Armstrong records knocked me out. Tep was crazy about Sidney Bechet. One time she said, 'You ought to listen to *this* guy.' It was Bix Beiderbecke on a 78 record, play-ing 'Sorry' and 'Since My Best Gal Turned Me Down'.

I was disappointed at first as it all sounded too busy. But next day I played it and listened to the melody lead – it was called CNT on the label. What a sound! It was a cornet! But I had never heard anything like it. The player didn't have the often-brassy, nanny-goat vibrato of many lead trumpets at the time.

I discovered no one else could make the sound that Bix made. Hoagy Carmichael said, 'It was like bullets hitting a bell.' Lots of copyists tried to get it (including me later) but no such luck. Louis Armstrong said, 'Ain't none of them play like him yet.'

Bix is probably my favourite artist in any medium. He was a musical genius – way ahead of his time. If I ever get stuck for ideas, or get depressed, on goes . . .

. . . a Bix record and I'm cured. (Unfortunately, Bix drank too much bad whisky and gin and died of alcoholism aged 28.)

In my 50s, when I was finally getting a real handle on the cornet and flugelhorn, I asked my aged mother, 'Where does this damned music thing come from? It's taking over from my drawing gene.' Mom's face darkened and that's when I learned that she'd been a musical prodigy, but had been stopped in her tracks.

Music has been such a big part of my life that it had to go into my book of adventures in animation. I think that musical timing has an awful lot to do with animation. I found that all the top animators have been musical in some way – or very musical.

ANIMATION IS LIKE MUSIC.
IT'S IN A SERIES – IT'S WHAT WENT BEFORE AND WHAT FOLLOWS
LIKE MUSIC, IT'S IN TRANSITION
IT'S WHERE YOU'RE COMING FROM
AND WHERE YOU'RE GOING.
AND IT'S LIKE A STORY

I think of animation as drawn music – clusters of drawings (or positions) are like clusters of notes. Like music it's in a series, it's where you put them. It's in transition, and it's like a story. It's transient but it makes a hell of an impact. It's where you're coming from and where you're going.

Again, 'It's all in the timing and the spacing.'

I find it's like the telling of a joke. It's *how* it's told and by *whom*. It's all in the timing. The same joke isn't funny at all when told academically – or by someone without good timing.

LEAVING SCHOOL

Back to being 15, at school and swamped in mathematics. One day we were introduced to the concept (and tool) of 'let X be the unknown factor'.

As X the unknown factor came in, my brain went out the window. And never came back.

I was fascinated by the idea, but I had no mental ability to use it in the math lessons.

When I was alone in Spain aged 20, I had no English reading material – until through the British Consulate I got a copy of Bertrand Russell and Alfred North Whitehead's classic

Principia Mathematica and read it cover to cover. It was very interesting but I still didn't understand anything.

However, in the middle of the book, I discovered that 'X as the unknown factor' was a profoundly philosophical concept. I'd sensed that before, but couldn't do anything with it, couldn't even do the school work.

So, let's sum up:

If I had believed the school authorities I had:

No artistic talent whatsoever

Very little music talent

A below-average brain.

I was trying very hard but my mind refused to budge. I went on strike. My marks had gone to hell and it was clear I would fail the junior matriculation. My parents realised it was over. So did I. Now I wouldn't even have the necessary academic qualifications to get into the Ontario College of Art.

Again my parents must have stepped in, and I had an interview with Fred Haines, the principal of the art college. He was a kindly man, known for his competent and pleasant land-scape watercolours. Apparently he was impressed with my work, thought I was 'a good citizen' and decided to make an exception in my case. I was accepted.

I went from hell to what I knew would be heaven. This was in 1948 and I had saved up enough money to take a Greyhound bus to Los Angeles, stay at the YMCA for two months and try to get inside the Disney studio. And then come back to my first year of art school!

For this last year at high school I had a kindly form teacher, Mr Hobbs, who recognised my situation and tried to encourage me through my failing efforts.

I WAS 16 OR 17 WHEN I DID MAIL SLOTS LIKE THIS FOR the YMCA and CARTOONS FOR "The Caliper," A MAGAZINE FOR PARAPLEGICS.

Coincidentally, we all had a government IQ test. I begged Mr Hobbs to tell me my results, which might explain my situation.

He said, 'We're not allowed to give out that information.' Being me, I persisted and he eventually let me know that I was 'just under average intelligence'.

This came as a kind of relief to me, that I just wasn't smart enough, but it wasn't accepted at home.

Many years later, when I was working in my studio in Soho Square in London, Mr Hobbs turned up at reception to see me. I was on a rush job and didn't go out to see him. Big regrets – Dick, you should have.

He said to the receptionist, 'Oh, I always knew he would be a big success like this.'

The photograph here shows my friend Richie Brown and me at age 16 or 17 with our Donald Duck and Bugs Bunny and Elmer Fudd puppet show – 'cartoon marionettes'. (We'd never be allowed to get away with using famous cartoon characters today, but those were naive days.)

Richie was very funny and a skilled voice talent. I was okay at it and we made good money at kids' parties and holiday events.

On the entertainment circuit we became friendly with the very tall (six foot seven inches) English magician Ernest Cavell.

Ernie was a distinguished-looking gentleman who had spent most of his life as a member of the Royal Canadian Mounted Police up in the Arctic wastes of Canada. He was known as 'the Wizard of the North'.

I drew a large portrait of this fascinating character and gave it to him.

During one of my Easter breaks from art college, Ernie said he and his assistant, an Inuit boy of 17, were going to drive down to Florida for two weeks to the race tracks. They invited me along. I thought there'd be lots to draw.

Ernie was Chairman of the National Horsemen's Benevolent and Protective Association, looking after the best interests of the jockeys. It was quite a sight to see him surrounded by those tiny men.

However, it turned out I wasn't interested in the race tracks or gambling and I couldn't get near the horses to draw. This excerpt from my letter home gives you the idea.

Miami, Florida
Mon 12 February

Dear Mom and Dad,
    This is the first time I have ever felt guilty about taking a vacation. Now that I am here I can't find any <u>real</u> reason for coming.

Charles J. McLennan

taking a vacation. Now that I am here, I can't seem to find any <u>real</u> reason for coming. It is wonderful down here, but when I think of all the work I could be doing — I feel miserable.

I'm getting quite a few drawings done, but it still bothers me. It seems awfully funny, that now, of all times, I should want to do a pile of work, but when I see all the rich easygoing people here, living in an impossible world of luxury, all bored, and accomplishing nothing.

I want to get away from it all. It's too fantastic. When there is so much for me to learn, I just can't completely relax and swim at nights in illuminated swimming pools, and bask on the sea shore with fat old men chewing cigars and spoilt kids who just sit and watch television in fancy hotels. I guess I seem silly — being so lucky to be able to take off school and get into tropical weather, and yet kick about it, but I

It is wonderful down here, but when I think of all the work I could be doing – I feel miserable.

I'm getting quite a few drawings done, but it still bothers me. It seems awfully funny that now, of all times, I should want to do a pile of work, but when I see all the rich, easy-going people here, living in an impossible world of luxury, all bored, and accomplishing nothing, I want to get away from it all.

It's too fantastic. When there is so much for me to learn, I just can't completely relax and swim at nights in illuminated swimming pools, and bask on the sea shore with fat old men chewing cigars and spoilt kids who just sit and watch television in fancy hotels.

I guess I seem silly – being so lucky to be able to take off school and get into tropical weather and yet kick about it, but I just feel that it's been nice, but time to get back to reality.

Reality arrived one early morning in the shape of all six foot seven inches of the Wizard of the North sliding into my bed, plastering me to the wall. I jumped up. I was off the bed and out the door in one swoop, grabbing my bag en route, and had to hitchhike 1,500 miles back up through the USA to Canada, in the middle of the northern winter.

It was scary as hell, going through the night in the Everglade swamps. You could hear creatures rustling on both sides of the road. Fortunately, there was an almost full moon, so I could be seen pretty clearly, and though there were few cars and trucks, they tended to pick you up. In those days, hitching rides wasn't dangerous as it is now.

I had just enough cash for food but only one jacket, and all I can really remember is freezingly empty roads and the Pennsylvania Mountains. It must have taken two days and two nights, up home to Toronto.

I never saw Ernie again.

OFF TO LA

Now I was out of my cage and in my own world.

Naturally, Mom and Dad were concerned about me going off alone to California for two months at age 15: Mom was great, but Dad threw a fit at the last minute to stop me. He was starting to do stuff like this, I imagine from pressure of work – also he was becoming more authoritarian as he grew older and I'm sure I was becoming more difficult.

In a crunch like this, Mom always came through for me, and she insisted I should go. I had a small bag and jumped on the bus.

It took either four days and five nights or five days and four nights non-stop to ride the Greyhound buses all the way from Toronto to Los Angeles. The first bus would go for eight hours (with comfort stops) then I'd get the overnight bus for eight hours, then another one for eight hours and then start all over again.

ARDENT "Y" ENTHUSIAST'S AMBITION IS TO GIVE DISNEY IDEAS

TYPICAL OF YOUTHS enjoying Y.M.C.A. activities is Richard Williams, 14, of Toronto, a cartoonist who hopes to be a "top" idea man for Walt Disney. Williams is on a "Y" swimming team, competes in inter-"Y" meets and is painting a mural at Central "Y" pool. The Y.M.C.A.-Y.W.C.A. drive for $2,121,000 will provide facilities for others

'Y. M.C.A. ARTIST, 14, PAINTING MERMAID PIN-UP ON 'Y' POOL'

It seemed endless: tedious, but thrilling and astonishing at the same time. America is huge! It is such an amazingly beautiful and contrasting land. Traffic was minimal too, all those years ago, and you really felt space. Giant space everywhere with magnificent mountains, valleys, deserts, forests – all on such a scale! And you can imagine I met some real characters along the way.

I got to Los Angeles some 2,520 miles later and landed at the YMCA on South Hope Street. (The 'Y' organisation really did provide me with stable centres for activities from when I was 5 years old. It was wholesome in its approach to youth and never pushed the religious element at you.)

The branch was situated near Figueroa Street, in what was then the tough part of Los Angeles. I loved everything: the city, downtown, the theatres, the atmosphere, the weather and the 'Y' itself, which had lots of room and an Olympic-size swimming pool.

Right away I took the bus out to Burbank and walked up and down along the long fence in front of the Disney studio – trying to figure out how to get in. No luck.

Over the following days I had quite a relationship with that fence, but I finally got inside!

I did have one contact in Los Angeles. Mom and Dad knew an advertising man called Charlie Hutchings and his wife Christine.

'Thanks Dad for writing Charlie Hutchings. He phoned me right away and I had dinner there. They are the sweetest people. Joe Reddy who handles publicity for Disney's wants me to come up to where the old films were made.'

I knew that Charlie was impressed with my work and had rung up the Disney publicity department. I wrote to Mom and Dad:

> **My luck hasn't run out yet. Charlie Hutchings knew somebody who knew somebody etc. who knew Joe Reddy who is in charge of Disney publicity, who wanted as a result to do a story on me. So I phoned Disney's and made an appointment to see him. I shot the old bull about coming all the way for the specific purpose of seeing the studios.**
>
> **Anyway they took me around the studio all morning and then to lunch, then all afternoon around the studio and then they did a story for the _Toronto Star._ It was the biggest day of my life. I met Walt (who was impressed – no kidding) and Bing Crosby as well as all the top men, Ward Kimball, Dick Kelsey who does all the _Fantasia_-like sequences such as the storm in _Bambi_ and all the beautiful stuff the studio puts out. Best of all I met Ray Williams, who did the cartoons for _Post, Colliers, New Yorker_ etc. He gave me a few drawings and an ashtray (which is a caricature of Ray).**

Until I read this letter, I was sure that I hadn't met Walt Disney. I can see why now. As a kid, I was only fascinated with the artists and I knew that Walt didn't really draw. But on seeing my letter the whole scene flashed back into my mind in detail.

Bing Crosby must have been there at that time to use his voice for the Narrator, Ichabod Crane and Brom Bones in _The Legend of Sleepy Hollow_. Bing Crosby had roomed with my hero Bix Beiderbecke when they worked with Paul Whiteman in the late 1920s. Bing said he learned everything from Bix. I wish I'd had the sense to ask him about Bix, but I was too much into showing my drawings to Disney. (Stories from the men who worked with Walt Disney about what he really did and what he was like will keep popping up as we go through this book.)

The sage advice I was given on this visit by the animator Dick Kelsey was a life changer:

> **ME: I want to be this terrific animator. What shall I do?**
> **DICK: Forget about animating. First learn to draw.**
> **ME: (_Showing my stuff again_) But I _do_ draw.**
> **DICK: Not this kind of stuff. I mean _really_ learn to draw. You can take up animating later, if you want to.**

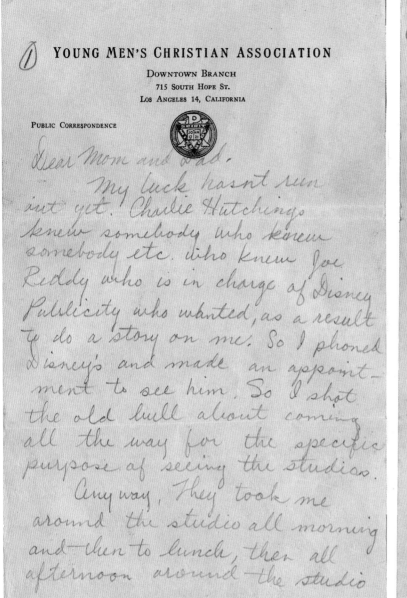

YOUNG MEN'S CHRISTIAN ASSOCIATION

Downtown Branch
715 South Hope St.
Los Angeles 14, California

Public Correspondence

Dear Mom and Dad,

My luck hasn't run out yet. Charlie Hutchings knew somebody who knew somebody etc. who knew Joe Reddy who is in charge of Disney Publicity who wanted, as a result to do a story on me. So I phoned Disney's and made an appointment to see him. So I shot the old bull about coming all the way for the specific purpose of seeing the studios.

Anyway, they took me around the studio all morning and then to lunch, then all afternoon around the studio

and then they did a story for the Toronto Star. So It was the biggest day of my life. I met Walt, (who was impressed – no kidding) and Bing Crosby as well as all the top men, Ward Kimball, Dick Kelsey, (who does all the Fantasia-like sequences such as the storm in Bambi and all the beautiful stuff the studio puts out. Best of all I met Ray Williams, who does the cartoons for Post, Colliers New Yorker etc. He gave me a few drawings and an ashtray (which is a caricature of Ray.)

I learned from Amid Amidi – when he was writing his book on the Disney animation genius Ward Kimball – that Dick Kelsey was Ward's art school teacher and Ward got Walt to bring Dick into Disney's.

How I regret not thanking Dick Kelsey forty years later, when I saw him again in the Disney canteen. If only I had broken away from the *Roger Rabbit* film entourage and run up to him. He gave me some of the best advice I ever received.

Can you imagine the effect all this had on my 15-year-old mind?

I've had several articles in the Canadian papers during my professional life but the strange thing is that the *Toronto Star* one never appeared.

I think it must be for the same reason that, when I was 14, radio interviewer Gordon Sinclair shook me and commanded, 'Stay here!'

I think it's very different now. I hope so.

Williams, Richard

TORONTO BOY, NO. 1 DISNEY FAN,
SCORES HIT IN STUDIO VISIT

Walt Disney got an interesting slant on his work and his studio through the eyes of a 15-year-old Canadian boy on his first visit to the Burbank home of Mickey Mouse, Donald Duck and the whole troupe of cartoon characters which have carried the Disney name and fame around the world.

At the same time, the boy---probably the No. 1 Disney fan on the continent---confirmed his long-range impressions of the animation wizard and his organization during a leisurely day-long meander through the artist's and animator's work shops, sound and camera rooms, executive offices and technical chambers, talking to top craftsmen, inspecting story boards and discussing story ideas and treatment and all the processes of animation.

He is Dick Williams, son of Mr. and Mrs. Ken Williams of 191 Golfdale Road, Toronto. Given his choice of vacation journeys, he elected Hollywood and a visit to the studio of cartoon wonders. Permission for the unusual freedom in the Disney plant was given young Williams because of his already intelligent knowledge of the producer's medium and methods.

The tall, blue-eyed youngster, himself a promising artist and professional puppeteer, is no mere callow movie fan. For years he has seen and studied every Disney picture. He has kept tabs on every development and trend in cartoon technique. He has followed the names and assignments of Walt's studio personnel. He has read every scrap of information he could find about the place where Mickey Mouse, Donald

---

Duck, Pluto and their comic pals cut their capers amidst Bambi and Thumper, Brer Rabbit and Bongo, Dumbo and Madame Upanova, Little Toot and Pecos Bill and the endless parade of characters who make screen animation history. And out of this fund of information, he could and did talk and listen knowingly to the cartoon wizards, who, on their part, also paid him respectful attention as representative of a vast audience age group.

Without being as brash as he might sound, Dick Williams says he's going to be a Disney man himself, when he completes his schooling. All his plans point that way. He has already taken the test formerly given applicants for animation jobs and scored an assistant's rating, with only his youth standing in the way of immediate action.

Among staffs artists he talked with in the studio are Dick Kelsey, who works directly with Disney on new projects and is now in advance research and story phases of "Hiawatha," one of Walt's most elaborate and costly projects; Roy Williams, who gave him a demonstration of cartooning in simple, basic line drawing; John Walbridge, idea man who explores character and comedy invention prior to animation, and who is just now working on "Alice in Wonderland." Young Dick got a big laugh out of the tea party sketches and the antics of the jabberwork on the "Alice" story boards.

Knowing Walt's preference for comedy in all his works, Dick wanted to know how he was going to contrive the proper amount of light and amusing fantasy in the strong dramatic legend of Hiawatha. He was reassured. Admitting a strong leaning toward the all-cartoon production he also quickly got Walt's viewpoint on the producer's recent variation in a combination of live and cartoon action.

- 2 -

What most amazed him was the extensive explorations on each feature picture in the story board sketches of suggested animation and background art. Here, in a couple hours' intensive explanation by the Disney artists, animators and dramatists, the young Canadian got the equivalent of a semester in pictorial dramatics at any college. Dick reciprocated with an especially articulate comment on the viewpoint and preferences of adolescent audiences toward the Disney entertainment product.

Williams was somewhat chastened but not discouraged by the quality, the quantity and the vast diversity of skills that go into a finished cartoon fantasy. The craftsmanship and artistry which put half a million separate drawings into a 70-minute feature, like "MELODY TIME" and "SONG OF THE SOUTH," for example and many more into such forthcoming features with music as "ALICE IN WONDERLAND," "THE THREE WISHES," a story of the little people of Ireland, and the projected "TREASURE ISLAND."

The young Torontan comes by his preferences and talents naturally. His mother, he says, was once a leading commercial artist of his native city. His father is an advertising man with Brigden's, Ltd. In drawing and painting, design and even simple animation, he is already well advanced.

He and his comrade, Richard Brown, have been putting on puppet show in Toronto for over a year, for schools and clubs, using characters modeled on the Disney figures, especially Donald Duck. Brown does the "squawk talk," while Dick manipulates the puppets and narrates.

Walt Disney accounts Dick Williams one of the most interesting you visitors he has ever had at the studio.

- 3 -

**The unpublished article –
'TORONTO BOY, NO. 1 DISNEY FAN,
SCORES HIT IN STUDIO VISIT'**

It was time to leave. I'd also done a lot of competitive swimming, clown diving for a 'Y' aquacade, and I'd heard, close-up, a lot of fine jazz: Red Nichols's band (a lot of the men who had played with Bix), Kid Ory and Rosy McHargue's Dixieland band, and early Chet Baker.

I was on my way home, this time instead of going across the top of the States and down, going along the bottom and up. Five days later I was in Toronto and ready for art school.

ART SCHOOL

The Ontario College of Art was next to the Art Gallery of Ontario and by chance I stumbled into a room full of Rembrandts.

Bursting into tears, I suddenly realised what art was all about – or at least started to realise what it was all about.

I was so happy to be in the art school, but it was a shock that in our foundation year there were about ten artists who drew better than those in the graduating year. It was an unusual thing – the beginner students' work was often mistaken for the work of the graduating class.

'Here's one of my first assignments at art school. "Go out into Toronto and come back with a drawing of part of the city." I'm pleased to see that at 15 I had patience, and understanding of perspective – something I'd need for animation problems later on.'

They were much older than me, but I saw that I had to pull my socks up and work hard.

For me, there were two superb teachers.

The first, Eric Freifeld, was a terrific draughtsman.

In one of my first life drawing classes, he looked at my drawing and announced to the entire class, 'Here's a clever little fellow who's never seen *anything*.'

After class I knocked on Eric's door.

'Sir, Sir, what shall I do?'

He said, 'Go – to – the – library – and study – Albrecht Dürer – for – two – years.'

Well, I didn't do the two years but I did study lots of Dürer, Holbein, Grünewald and all that German analytical art.

It was the perfect antidote to the cartoons, comic books and American illustrations I'd been raised on.

You can never study enough anatomy; I never studied enough early on, but filled it in as I went through the years.

The second great teacher in the school was Fred Hagan, who taught drawing the figure in costume. He also ran the lithography shop, working on printing from the lithographic stones. This wasn't part of my course, but I managed to do it anyway. The whole process of lithography – from grinding the stones in order to draw on them and treating them with acid, to printing from them on the big presses – taught me the patience and systemisation that would aid me later in the whole animation process.

Fred had often run the arts and crafts programme in the summers at the YMCA Camp Pine Crest and he'd been kind and encouraging to me when I was there from ages 6 to 10.

We were to become lifelong friends, even after I was mostly based in England.

But Fred was another tough cookie. He was both challenging and stimulating.

He had invented his own private art language, the sort that academics often develop. Nobody understood what he was saying; certainly I never did.

Years later, when I visited Fred at his home back in Canada, I was sitting with his wife Liz on the sofa as Fred was tending the fire.

I said to Liz, 'You know, I never understood what he was saying. Do you?'

Liz said, 'No, but look at him. I just fancy him.'

The most promising students always gravitated to Fred and his family and we were treated as friends, with great hospitality. When I left the school, Fred let me work in his own workshop using his stones and printer.

The foundation year included sculpture – working in clay. This was my most difficult subject because my work tends to be linear, not solid chunkiness.

We had a fine English sculptor with terrible breath teaching us, who kept leaning in to me as I pushed the clay around. 'Put it down and leave it there, Williams. Put it down and leave it there.'

This was because my early exposure to commercial art caused me to always have a surface polish to my work. So, again, it was an antidote.

FRED
BY DICK
SALT SPRING
15 MAY 94

49

In the end, I did a good job, but I *still* have to say to myself, 'Put it down and leave it there, Williams. Put it down and leave it there.'

After the foundation year, my parents insisted that I go into the three-year advertising art course and not into the 'pretentious longhair' drawing and painting department. Advertising art paid for everything we had and did – and a 'fine art' approach was regarded as a part-time occupation at best.

I got high marks right away, but I was getting bored with the advertising approach. I already knew how to do lettering, layouts, etc. (The 'fine art' attitude always was that if you could do good lettering then you couldn't be a 'real' artist. BALONEY. Dürer, Holbein and Titian all did beautiful lettering. It was the less skilled modern artists who couldn't.)

I still knocked off cartoons for fun and money but I was increasingly going to the life classes in the drawing and painting department.

The 2ND YEAR AT ART COLLEGE MY FRIEND, BRUCE WALKER and I DREW THIS SATIRE ON the SCHOOL STAFF FOR the YEAR BOOK.

OUTRAGEOUS, BUT WE DIDN'T GET INTO TROUBLE FOR IT.

IN the CENTRE IS FREDERICK HAINES, the KINDLY PRINCIPAL WHO WAIVED the RULES TO LET ME INTO the COLLEGE.

I FEEL I NEED A KICK UP the ASS FOR CARICATURING HIM.

COMING ATTRACTION (ON the BIJOU POSTER) FOR NEW PRINCIPAL IS L·A·C· PANTON, WHO HAD TOLD ME I HAD NO TALENT WHATSOEVER. TROUBLE AHEAD...

I became the favourite of the head of the advertising art department. He was Fred Finley (an Australian artist who my parents knew). He'd been (or was) a competent illustrator specialising in masculine figures for advertising. He was a fit man who wore a suit and tie.

He was always talking about the 'planes' of the human figure: 'Get the planes.' I was suspicious of this approach – sure, there are the planes but we've got to understand the *inner* structure in order to show the planes on top.

He confided in me, 'Go to New York and be successful, you can make lots of money and you'll find lots of girls that way and you'll have a whale of a time.' I didn't think that was exactly my motivation to be an artist.

The problem with the advertising and illustration course was that it was neat and clean and superficial – surface work. I needed to get my hands dirty, I wanted to get below the surface and I knew that endless drawing was the way forward.

A famous life drawing teacher of the time said something like, 'You've got several thousand bad drawings in you, so you might as well get busy getting rid of them.' That's pretty negative and not very encouraging but he had a point and I definitely got busy.

Aged 16, I had earned enough cash from my dog food ads to buy a small used convertible Morris Minor car. 'Used' was the word, as I bought it from a drunk whom Dad knew. Now I could get around the place easily. Also (thanks to Grandad's inventiveness) our large 'pop-up' puppet stage folded neatly into it.

I also continued to hear a lot of live music. I found a copy of my birth certificate recently and was shocked to see I was born in 1932, not 1933 – so I was a year older than I had thought.

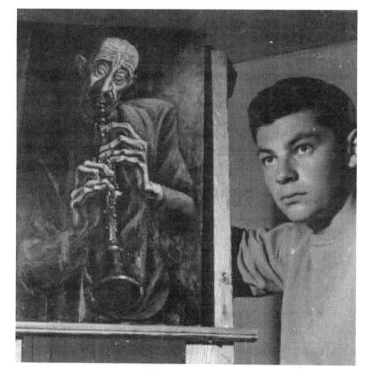

With my painting of Pee Wee Russell

Then I realised it was a forgery I'd made (altering the three to two) in order to appear old enough to get into jazz venues.

The top American groups came to the Colonial Tavern in Toronto and I heard my first jazz band live and up close: Muggsy Spanier and His Dixieland Band. Words fail me. Muggsy played the cornet like a drummer, with blazing, bouncing tempos. He had a punching beat which drove the band like a boxer.

I went there nearly every night, transfixed – and in the intervals I managed to talk to the players. Muggsy wasn't talkative, but when I asked him if he'd played with Bix, he replied, 'Everything they said about him was true!'

I heard many of the greats in the Colonial and mostly up close: Louis Armstrong, Sidney Bechet, Jimmy McPartland, Pee Wee Russell, Wild Bill Davison, Georg Brunis, Omer Simeon, Joe Sullivan, the young Ruby Braff. It was wonderful. I was so lucky.

I still found time for advertising work. When I was 16 or 17 my dad would often take me to work at an ad agency on Saturdays. They held the important account of B/A – British American Oil – and I would help with artwork and lettering for presentations with the art director, Buzz Walker.

In those days we used water-based poster colour. I noticed Buzz would never bother to clean his brush, he'd just put it down and picked up a new one every time. When I asked him why he didn't just pop it in the water and wipe it, he said, 'I know what's worth more – my time or the brushes.'

Welcome to the values of the advertising world, Dick. (I ended up with quite a collection of fine brushes.)

Through Dad, they got me to design a cartoonish storyboard for a colour TV commercial for B/A Oil. Surprisingly, they approved it and put it in production.

There were no animation studios in Toronto then, but they contacted a tiny new company thirty miles away called Graphic Associates, made up of three guys who had split from the National Film Board of Canada.

They were experienced in cut-out animation, moving jointed paper around, so we did it together. I did all the artwork and George Dunning (later known for directing *Yellow Submarine*) directed it and helped me animate it. It was successful and, as far as I know, it was the first colour animated commercial done in Canada.

When it came to developing it, there were no laboratories in Toronto who could handle 16 mm colour film, so George had to fly to New York with the exposed negative, wait for the combined sound prints and then fly back to Toronto.

I learned a lot from George and we became friends. He and his two business partners had built a magnificent place on a cliff outside Toronto near a village called Kleinburg.

George the animator and John the financier lived up top in separate ends of the studio/home and Jim McKay, the second animator, lived with his wife and two kids down in the valley below.

Every working day Jim would walk up from the valley to work in the studio and walk down home again. I noticed that he got a lot more work done than the two who lived in the house. Even though they were far apart in the house, life and work tended to blur together.

I always try to work in a separate place from the home, even if it's just crossing a little bridge to a garage – work seems to be more successful if there is some sort of break away from where you live.

I now have a good working set-up in our basement when I need to be home, but my present workroom in Aardman Animations is ideal. I do some travelling to work and then step into silence and privacy. It's like stepping into my mind, and I know if the phone ever rings it's going to be Mo. It's the best situation I've ever had.

George Dunning had a great effect on me. The National Film Board charter allowed for *all* kinds of film, including experimental or 'personal' work. For example, Norman McLaren drew or scratched right on the negative and 'drew' his own sound effects on the optical track.

George showed me personal stuff he had done with no narrative. There was one strange surreal piece of a ball in slow motion going down a stairway in space – with no attempt at what the Hollywood guys call 'squash and stretch'. The ball was hard – and the feeling was the opposite to a cartoon. Very contemplative – hard to explain. He'd also done some animation of a horse on plates of glass, painting with oil paint directly on the glass plates, often with the images dissolving one into another.

This opened my mind. It made an indelible effect on my lifelong approach to animation: a completely non-Disney or non-cartoon or non-conventional way of thinking. (George also had no registration pegs, guides or whatever.)

At around the same time, the UPA Studios burst on the scene with *New Yorker*-ish sophisticatedly stylist shorts such as *Gerald McBoing-Boing* and my lifelong favourite *Rooty Toot Toot*, designed and directed by John Hubley.

Rooty Toot Toot is the story (with a great jazz track) of the song 'Frankie and Johnny' – Frankie shoots her lover Johnny dead and the film takes place during her trial for murder. The celebrated animator Art Babbitt animated two thirds of the film, with the defendant Frankie and her lawyer dancing *en pointe* like ballet dancers. A fantastic piece of work!

The combined effect of George's experiments and UPA's artistically sophisticated approach turned me off the beautifully developed but – to me and others – out-of-date Disney approach to the medium.

But as we will later see – not forever!

UPA eventually got cut off in its prime by the McCarthyite blacklist, and left-wing artists like John Hubley escaped to New York to work independently.

I loved John's shorts (he won three Oscars for them) and I knew him a bit, much later in life, not realising he'd directed my favourite short ever – *Rooty Toot Toot*.

In my second year of art school Graphic Associates moved to Toronto so, alongside my studies, I did bits and pieces of animation for George.

By then I didn't seriously consider being an animator, and I was also becoming more and more uncomfortable in the commercial art department.

I turned 17, the summer came, I got my little car fixed up and my friend from advertising Bruce Walker and I decided we'd drive down through the States to Mexico. Bruce knew somebody down there and I had just discovered the great Mexican muralists Rivera, Siqueiros and Orozco. Amazing work from another world.

Plus – what did we know about Mexico? Very little.

We stopped off in New York City en route to go to the Metropolitan Museum of Art and also to go to Eddie Condon's jazz restaurant/bar.

The Condon band was a favourite of mine. It didn't matter who was in it, they always had a very together swinging band sound – even though it was all improvised. They always had my favourite players.

I felt so privileged. It was quite dark but I managed a few drawings.

Then we drove down through the south to New Orleans along Lake Pontchartrain. It was so *hot*! I'd never experienced heat like that. It was so humid that if you put a trumpet mouthpiece on your lip to play, it would just slide off. How did the musicians manage? Air conditioning wasn't exactly common in those days.

In the late 1940s and 1950s, the 'rediscovery' and revival of the early foundations of jazz and folk music was centred mostly in New Orleans, the 'birth-place' of jazz. Some of the early players were still alive and being recorded just in time. Some of them had to have instruments (and teeth) bought for them.

I had heard clarinettist George Lewis on records (with pioneer trumpeter Bunk Johnson) and we were able to get to where he was playing.

They started with 'Bugle Boy March'. The trumpeter Percy Humphrey fluffed the bugle call introduction and then the band kicked in. After eight bars I thought, 'Dick, forget it.'

George Lewis

I don't know what it was, but it was something very different. They weren't virtuosos like I'd been hearing, but this was a real ensemble voice, with a marvellous beat.

I can't describe it . . . bursting with heart, joy, freedom, 'soul' – a combination of all that. It was wonderful.

Then we drove across the US into the Mexican desert. The road (in those days) was narrow, rough and full of pot-holes. We were headed towards Mexico City, about two days' drive away. Of course, it was very hot, but dry heat, and we had the top down on the convertible. As the evening sun was about to go down the car stopped. No reason. It just decided to not go any more, and came to a quiet stop.

We sat there, stunned. I was no mechanic and I had no idea what to do. Bruce knew less than me.

There was desert on our left and hills on the right. At the top of the hills were some small white buildings. When we looked closely, we could see men in white with sombreros starting to come down towards us. They didn't look friendly.

It occurred to the both of us that we were in the middle of nowhere and we could easily be made to disappear, as could the car. As the men came closer, we could see they were carrying sticks of some kind.

I don't know where on earth this came from, but I said, 'It's – the – carburettor.' Now, I didn't know where or what the carburettor was or did. I got out and opened the bonnet, found a silver tube, fiddled with the top of it and some sliding bits, shut the bonnet tight, sat down, started the car and we drove off as the definitely hostile men came within range.

I still don't know about what the carburettor is or does. I have no explanation, I just know that the whole event scared the hell out of me.

That night, or the next one, we had the opposite experience. We found a tiny village and a place to stay.

At two or three in the morning we were awakened by the sound of two guitarists out in the yard playing mariachi music. Then other guitarists started to arrive and join in. It was amazing. They were playing for the joy of it, obviously friends. They ended up with nine guitars all blending marvellously.

I tried to stay awake but I'd been driving all day. I fell asleep and reawakened to the sound of a single trumpet playing on top of the nine guitars.

He was phenomenal, world class, a master musician. There was no trace of the amateur or semi-professional and the whole group was just terrific.

I thought, how many people are like this, unknown virtuosos in parts of the world where they are never discovered?

They played until dawn, then presumably went back into the hills and farms or whatever. I felt so privileged, and so stupid that I couldn't speak Spanish.

Mexico blew my 17-year-old mind.

I realised how big, varied, rich and colourful the world is. I've been to Mexico three times in my life and it is the most interesting country I've visited. Everything is heightened. The colours are brighter, the contrasts are greater, the air and the light are so different from the north.

I was knocked out by seeing the actual works of the three great political muralists: Diego Rivera, David Alfaro Siqueiros and especially José Clemente Orozco. Also by a more recent and more abstract painter with wonderful colours, Rufino Tamayo. It was like the skin being taken off the eyes.

What the hell does all this have to do with animation, you may ask? Answer: For me, a lot.

It blew away all my preconceptions about art and opened my mind to new possibilities. Nothing has to be done the way it's been done before! Who's to say it has to be done this way or that way?

Back to art school – with a vengeance.

LEARNING FAST

The Captive: **lithograph**

In my middle years I was playing in New York with a classically trained jazz trombonist who had graduated from the prestigious Juilliard School of Music.

I said, 'Boy, it must have been marvellous to be there. You must have learned an enormous amount.'

He grunted. 'Yeah . . . from my fellow students.'

He had a point.

In our school's drawing and painting course there were some real talents, and I was absorbing everything I could. As far as I could see, the most talented student was Graham Coughtry.

I started hanging around with Gray. He was two years older than me, 19 to my 17, quite a difference between those ages at that time/stage, but we got along well and became friends.

He said, 'What on earth are you doing in the advertising course?'

I started to paint with him in his folks' basement. With my little car I was mobile, and we could nip in and out of the school to his place outside Toronto's limits.

I was very influenced by Gray and unconsciously started working in his 'style'. He was very accomplished and his work was already distinctive, strong and sensuous.

Mom had warned me years before, 'Forget about style, just do the work and a style will naturally occur.' Right on, Mom.

Graham was also very musical, funny, a good mimic and could sing just like an authentic blues singer. He could hear a chorus by a terrific player on record and sing it right back at you. We loved the same periods of jazz. I was coming along on the cornet and Gray was messing with the trombone.

These were great days for me. Between 17 and 18 I could feel myself making huge steps forward. It was probably the biggest and fastest development and improvement of my working life. It's evident in the change in the work.

I still pulled in the marks in the commercial course but who cared? I hadn't cared about my previous marks either.

I was drawing non-stop, in the street, on the bus, on streetcars, in the park – and getting in to extra life drawing classes and the lithography workshop, and practically living in Graham's basement.

Gray shared his knowledge of paints and canvases, varnishes, gesso, etc. and often referred to a book, *Materials of the Artist* by Max Doerner, which he thoroughly understood. Gray was a very good colourist and he opened my mind to colour. He showed me how to paint.

My first picture (naturally of three musicians) used El Greco's method of working on a dark green ground and making an underpainting of the figures using egg tempera – so they looked like white ghosts – then glazing over the top with layers of oil colours, which gave it a translucent quality. This method was used by many of the Renaissance masters.

The Art Gallery of Ontario held an annual exhibition of the Royal Canadian Academy of Arts and any artist could submit their work. Graham and I both had our pictures accepted, and this first painting of mine sold immediately. That didn't hurt.

We were also friends with a fellow student, Georgine Strathy, a superb natural draughts-person. She drew like an angel. She became the top fashion artist in the country.

Georgine's boyfriend was Michael Snow, who was stuck in the industrial design course. Mike was four or five years older than me. He was always 'far out' in his artwork, but I was more struck by his astonishing natural talent as a musician. It was like magic – he could play polyrhythmic piano exactly like Jelly Roll Morton (a feat in itself) and then switch styles through to bebop.

I used to beg him to play with the jazz band at the college ball and I'd stand there amazed as he made the piano sound like a full swinging band. He was so brilliant that again I thought, I don't really have much talent.

Mike played in Ken Dean's professional Dixieland band (with Bud Hill, a trombonist) and a great thrill for me was to listen to them practise in Mike's Rosedale living room.

Twenty years later, Mike visited me in my London studio at a time when I was playing cornet a lot. I always kept my cornet alongside my drawing desk. I had to go upstairs for something, then I heard amazing sounds coming from downstairs. Mike was all over that damned horn.

Go back to Grade One, Dick.

When I last checked, Mike had become the most celebrated artist in Canada.

Graham, of course, was always way ahead of me in discovering other artists – William Blake, Stanley Spencer, Edward Hopper, Käthe Kollwitz, Andrew Wyeth, Ben Shahn, etc. – but I was moving fast. It was exhilarating.

I was drinking in knowledge, doing hard work, playing lots of music and having fun. The school's atmosphere was free, but serious. Then the head of the college, who everyone liked, resigned.

Shock, horror! He was replaced by L. A. C. Panton, my high school art department head. The atmosphere changed as Panton tried to turn the college (which was full of mature students) into a high school. He irritated both students and teachers.

He put in high school rules, had people signing in and out with strict times of arrivals and exits. Everyone tried to avoid him, but he didn't affect my concentration at all.

I was drawing people wherever I went. I had a black 'Bible-like' sketch book with covers that helped to disguise my scribbling. I was drawn to the rough downtown area, in reaction against the squeaky-clean suburban life and advertising approach. They called this kind of art 'social realism' at the time.

I stumbled into a large Pentecostal church, which announced 'speaking in tongues' on Wednesday nights.

I could sit unobserved on a balcony and look down to draw the people.

They had four or five young girls playing hymns on cornets with angelically innocent tones – beautiful.

The rest turned out to be not so innocent.

Sister Fern Huffstutler, a large, imposing revivalist preacher, arrived from the American South to lead the crusade.

I was fascinated by the whole thing and did several drawing sessions of the mostly elderly congregation. One night I went down and sketched them up close as they gyrated and rolled on the ground, crying out 'in tongues'.

An 'officer' efficiently slithered among them in their trances, whispering 'Ten dollars for Sister Fern, ten dollars for Sister Fern.'

I decided to use my sketches and make a very big painting of the whole operation seen from above.

Sister Fern, 1952

Later on, I made a lithograph of the painting. (The original is in some Canadian art gallery.)

When the annual Royal Canadian Academy of Arts's Exhibition of Canadian Art came round again to the Art Gallery of Ontario, both Graham and I were again accepted. My entry was this picture: *Where the Healing Waters Flow*.

'I decided to make a large black and white lithography copy of my oil painting.
You draw directly on to a stone slab with a waxy crayon. It's a complex hand printing job and you can make copies. They come out flopped, left to right.'

It caused quite a fuss, partly because of its social content.

At the private view the cultural gentry were all there. I was standing near the painting when Mr Norris – the woodworking teacher from my vocational school who had disapproved of my Ivan Yurpee shows – came up to me and said, 'I want to apologise to you. I'm so sorry. I had no idea.'

I was still standing by the painting, talking to Will Ogilvie, a fine artist and part-time teacher at the college, when striding across toward us came L. A. C. Panton, RCA, OSA.

He said to Will, 'This boy is a genius!'

I made myself scarce. Panton obviously hadn't recognised me. I guess it was the physical difference between being 14 or 15 and 19.

There was some trouble at home with my dad, as I wasn't following the script any more. I mostly lived in the basement and ate at the other end of the kitchen with my back to Mom, my 5-year-old brother Tony and Dad. This was so he didn't have to look at me.

He was suffering from great pressure at work, although he was becoming very successful. I think what summed up my home situation was Dad telling me, 'You are a guest in this house.'

I was coming up to my graduation year – one year to go. I told Mom and Dad that I was wasting my time in the commercial department and needed to switch courses so that I'd have at least one year to study anatomy and the figure, and get more painting in while I had the chance. As by now I was paying all the fees myself I got their reluctant agreement.

My favourite teachers backed me but said I would have to get permission from – guess who.

I made the appointment to see the head and rolled up in front of L. A. C. Panton's desk.

I explained that I had won small scholarships and had top marks for the three years I'd been at the college (studying commercial art) and that since I was concentrating on the human figure I needed to switch to drawing and painting, as this would be my last chance to really study before I went out into the world to earn my living.

Long silence.

'I will allow you to switch courses for your final year.'

'Oh, thank you very much.'

'But, you will forfeit your chance at the big scholarship.'

(Graham and I were favourites to win it: $1,500 – a fortune at that time.)

'I understand.'

'And, you will not graduate.'

'Oh, I see. Yes.'

'And,' (with a little smile) 'you will never be allowed to teach.'

'I see. Will I get anything at all?'

'Well, we'll give you a piece of paper saying you've attended the college for four years.'

I think I said, 'I see. Well, if it's a question of either learning or getting a piece of paper, I'll choose to do the learning.' I left the office, vowing: I'll get you one day, you bugger!

BACK IN LA

I was 18 now and working in my teacher Fred Hagan's lithography workshop. I'd become friendly with Carl Bell, who was an enormous Disney fan and wanted to spend his life working at the Disney studio. (He later succeeded, and was also elected the maximum number of times to represent animation as a governor of the Academy of Motion Picture Arts and Sciences. Success.)

It was three years since my life-changing visit to the Disney studio and I was now so deeply into painting and drawing that I was a bit snobby about Disney stuff.

Carl said he was going to take the bus or train to Los Angeles to try to get inside the Disney studio. I had nothing planned for the summer and I still had my little banged-up Morris Minor convertible car. I told Carl that if we could treat it as a painting trip I was up for driving him there.

We had a magnificent trip across the startling vistas of the continent, with the only scary incident being both of us falling sound asleep with me only waking up as we crashed across the desert cacti at a forty-five-degree angle from the only road, half a mile behind us.

We ended up in Los Angeles at my familiar downtown YMCA.

I don't know how he did it, but Carl got us invited to a pre-release press screening of the not-quite-finished *Peter Pan*.

We were waiting outside the screening room with the journalists when I got my second (and last) viewing of Walt Disney.

On this occasion we didn't speak; he was busy mesmerising an attractive red-headed journalist from *Look* magazine. She was dressed in green and Walt had her up against the wall, almost nose to nose, transfixed as he 'Svengalied' her, telling a story from the yet-to-be-made *Lady and the Tramp*.

He said, 'And then the dog goes up the stairs to the baby's room and we wonder if the baby is in danger, and what's going to happen.' And then . . . and then . . . and *then* . . .

'Oh, Mr Disney! Mr Disney! . . . Oh, Mr Disney!'

I was kind of shocked but years later I realised he was just doing his job. And boy, was he doing it well. She was entranced, hanging on every word.

The guys all told me Walt was always trying story stuff out on anybody who was around, didn't matter who – kids, postmen, carpenters, anyone.

Fifty-five years later, when I was on the publicity tour for *Who Framed Roger Rabbit*, I was interviewed by Bob Thomas, an old professional journalist who'd been everywhere and seen and done everything, and who wrote a studio-approved biography of Walt.

The great animator Milt Kahl had told me, 'If you want to know what Walt was really like, read Bob Thomas's book. That'll give you a good idea. It's a very accurate picture of him.'

When Bob finished interviewing me about the *Rabbit* film, I grabbed the door handle and shut the door.

'Bob, I can't let this opportunity go. I really want to interview *you*.'

To start, I told him about the *Look* magazine woman I had seen fifty-five years ago, and he said, 'Oh sure, that red hair and green dress – that was Marsha.' (Or something like that.) '*Look* magazine – yeah.'

I said, 'I'm dying to ask you – what really was it about Disney? All those great guys – they all say *he* was the genius – and they all knew it. Was he the conceiver, the director, the story man, what?'

Bob's answer: 'Actor! A great actor! As good as Chaplin – but not in public. Only for his men (and not as 'Uncle Walt' on TV). He had a phenomenal memory and could act out anything for his artists; they all said that it was always so good that they could never match his performance.'

Later on, all of the great guys I knew confirmed this.

Milt Kahl always told me, 'When Walt died, we lost our best man.'

Back to *Peter Pan*:

What we saw was fascinating – one-third of the picture was still unfinished. Two-thirds of it was in finished colour with finished soundtrack, but the other one-third was rough pencil animation without numbers on drawings flashing around with a single-piano guide soundtrack.

I was stunned by the rough animation, but when the finished colour shots appeared, my interest dropped, although the colour styling and backgrounds were excellent. The rough stuff was more vital and intriguing. I'm afraid this is pretty much always true. An 'inside' look at the working process is somehow more compelling than the polished, finished item.

Michelangelo's unfinished *Slaves* are somehow even greater than his finished sculptures.

Why is a planning drawing more interesting than a finished painting of the same thing? People say, 'Don't finish it, you'll ruin it!' They also say, 'It's great that it isn't quite finished. It's even better than it would be if it was finished.'

Somehow the 'rough' is intimate – the thinking is showing. People say this is true of our film *The Thief and the Cobbler – A Moment in Time* (in the reconstruction made by the Academy of Motion Picture Arts and Sciences).

In animation, when hand-tracing of the cels stopped and the Xerox process of scanning the rough animation drawings started, the obvious looseness was very attractive – drawings that walked and talked.

Milt Kahl said they were always trying to persuade Walt to film the rough drawings, but Walt told him, 'No, the public like that slick traced line.'

The first film where the drawings were Xeroxed was *One Hundred and One Dalmatians*. Art director Ken Anderson was the designer of the film and was responsible for Xeroxing the background drawings in order to fuse and unify the animation drawings with the backgrounds.

The film was a big hit – but Walt hated it. He told Ken, 'That's not Disney!'

Ken had put together a marvellously functioning team who had done the work and Walt told him to personally fire them all. Ken was terrifically upset, fired them, dived into his swimming pool and had a massive heart attack.

Walt came to see him in the hospital and persuaded him to come back when he recovered and just work on anything he wanted – with never any pressure to complete or supervise anything, ever.

Ken's doctor told him to regularly visit a large group of beautiful trees to help him recover. It took a while but it worked.

Once, when I visited Ken, I said, 'What great colour you have in your work. Why don't they get that colour in the final result?'

Ken said, 'Don't ask me!'

Then he told me about the switch to Xeroxing.

The Xerox process saved all the expensive tracing and, for financial reasons, continued in all the productions from then on.

That *Peter Pan* rough screening had a hell of an influence on me – so I worked rough on as many productions as I could: on *A Christmas Carol*, *The Charge of the Light Brigade* and many others.

FINAL YEAR

My final year at the college was wonderful. I had access to all the models and facilities and felt completely at home. I could feel myself improving daily.

At my actual home, I lived mostly in the basement, which had a garden door, so I could come and go without disturbing the family.

I was improving on the cornet, improvising with friends, listening to lots of great music and doing lots of reading. I guess you could say I was discovering the 'cultural world'. I knew I was preparing myself for what I wanted to do – some sort of 'figure' art with music alongside.

Because Gray and I were both facile at capturing people's likenesses, we were selected to draw free, quick portraits of people at special events (I guess to represent the college).

Once we were sent to a convention of top medical doctors – to a gigantic mansion in Hoggs Hollow just outside the city limits. The first thing we noticed was the fabulously expensive cars surrounding the building.

We were to make instant portraits as the famous doctors ate lunch, and I looked forward to hearing the interesting conversations as we sketched.

Guess what they all talked about? Money. Cars.

COLLEGE IS OVER

I have a very clear memory of standing alone behind a glass wall, looking down into the theatre where the Ontario College of Art graduation ceremony was taking place.

The celebrated Canadian novelist Robertson Davies was the guest speaker.

'I thought, what can I say to you all about art? Then I realised that I couldn't say anything better about it than what's in these paperback books I bought on the way to this event.'

He threw thirty or forty books into the audience. They were copies of *The Horse's Mouth* by Joyce Cary, the British novelist who was hailed internationally at that time as the new Dickens.

I had already read the book and loved it.

Watching my friends graduate with honours and my pal Graham Coughtry walk off with the big scholarship gave me a strange feeling.

'I don't know if I fit here. But it's a big world. I'll be fine. I'm off.'

What I couldn't know was that three years later that very same novelist Joyce Cary would be approving my drawings for my first film, *The Little Island.* He was being shown them by his son Tristram Cary, one of the top film composers in England, who would create the film's soundtrack.

(When I read *The Horse's Mouth* I took it all very seriously, and obviously so did Robertson Davies. Later on, Tristram said to me, 'You know it's a satire, don't you? Dad wrote it as a satire.' So that's how two provincial minds in the Colonies misunderstood it.)

THE ROCKIES

Graham wanted to take his scholarship money and go to Europe for a year to see the great art museums, and I had saved up enough money to be able to do the same.

Gray had heard about a tiny Spanish island in the Mediterranean called Ibiza where artists had gone before the war. We decided we'd go there first, after our Canadian summer ended, and then travel round the European art museums.

That summer Fred Hagan, our teacher and friend, was going to be a temporary forest ranger in the Rocky Mountains in Alberta, stopping for two or three weeks with his family in the 'forest shelters'. We decided to do a painting trip, following them and taking over their shelters as they moved on.

My little Morris Minor car was showing lots of wear and tear by now but I figured it would take us across Canada and maybe back. Whether it would get up the mountains would be another story . . . .

So off we went, down into the United States, past Chicago, back up to Canada and across the prairies to the Rockies in Alberta, drawing along the way. Everything was great until we hit the impossibly high mountains.

They were so steep and twisting that we could only stay in first gear. The car couldn't carry the weight of two people.

Gray had to keep jumping in and out of the car, running alongside till it wasn't so steep, then jumping back in. Though there were few cars around in those days, they still piled up grumpily behind us. The road was so narrow that no one could pass.

It seemed obvious that the car would never make it back home, nor even up to Jasper National Park or the Great Glacier, but with Graham running alongside, jumping in and out, we finally made it.

We got to a 'shelter' up the side of the mountain which had a roof, cots for us to sleep in, a cooking stove and an outside wooden shack/toilet. We pitched our tent alongside it and had a great space to paint. Our tent was narrow with just enough room for two cots.

Gray must have been out somewhere, when I woke up one morning to find two brown bears coming right up towards me inside the tent. I was outside in a flash.

They were large cubs and I called out to warn Gray. This was really dangerous, because the mother was bound to be nearby. However, they just seemed curious to poke around and then left. Fortunately for us, their mom never showed up.

We saw no one for days, except when we hiked down to the Great Glacier, where there were a few people.

What on earth was I doing painting a self-portrait like this when I was in a shelter high up in the Rocky Mountains?

I guess I was asking myself, 'What kind of artist do I want to become?' Certainly not an advertising one!

I think I was trying to look past the impermanence of the advertising culture that I was raised in and surrounded by and that I had benefitted from . . . yet I wanted something else.

But I was also unsure about the art world.

One day at noon, way, way down the mountain on the road far below, two large buses arrived and stopped. The doors opened and out came what we thought were about 200 indigenous people, in full regalia. They were followed by several Mounties and a lot of equipment.

'It's a movie! They're making a movie down there! Crazy! Way out here in the wilds of the mountains!'

After a while, we could see a tiny shape coming up towards us. It took the man a long time as it was so steep. As he got closer, we saw he was dressed like a cartoon version of a film director.

He had jodhpurs and boots, breeches, hat, sunglasses. I couldn't resist, and started drawing him as he got closer and closer. He was a pure Hollywood figure.

'Hey, you guys! Can I use your shithouse?'

'Sure, help yourself.'

He disappeared inside as I frantically kept sketching him.

When he came out, he said, 'I'm Mervyn LeRoy, the guy who made *The Wizard of Oz*. We're making a remake of *Rose Marie* with Howard Keel and Ann Blyth. Why don't you guys come down and have a hot chicken box lunch?'

We jumped at it. We'd been dining on beans, tomato soup and crackers.

I kept drawing when he wasn't looking, so I had a few pretty accurate pictures.

Well, he was great with us. For some reason I kept those sketches for years in Mom and Dad's basement.

Now we go to forty years later. I have a wonderful kind friend, Tony Walton, who is a distinguished stage and costume designer and film art director living in New York.

For years I would turn up in NYC and stay in his back room, trying not to step on all the movie stars who were always coming in and out.

Tony's wife, Gen LeRoy, had previously been married to a man called Warner LeRoy. Tony and Gen were bringing up Gen's daughter Bridget LeRoy, whom I've known since she was 2. A really bright girl.

One day, when she was about 17, she mentioned that her grandad Mervyn LeRoy had made *The Wizard of Oz*.

'Mervyn LeRoy is your grandfather?'

I told her about our crazy encounter in the Rockies. Unbelievably, Mom had kept my drawings of him, so Bridget has them now.

Come September, Gray and I coasted down the mountains to Banff, and the car, on its last legs, just made it down on the flats to the desert on the other edge of Calgary, where it barely made it to a garage.

The garage guys fixed it up as best they could but said, 'This will never get you to Toronto.'

While we were absorbing this, the main garage guy came out, pointed to a scruffy older fellow in a chequered shirt waiting in the corner of the gas station and said, 'That man over there is quite interested in buying this thing as a birthday present for his 16-year-old daughter. How much do you want for it?'

I said, 'Anything he wants to give us.'

I think it was fifty dollars (quite a lot in those days). And he puttered happily away in the car towards Calgary.

The gas station man said, 'You know, that guy's a millionaire.'

I bought a pair of hiking boots – I don't remember what Graham got – and we started hitchhiking back across the continent. 2,500 miles to go. Fortunately, it was still warmish at the end of summer and we managed to pick up various lifts.

I don't fully recall how and where we slept but I do remember trying to sleep in an abandoned truck on a cliff overlooking Medicine Hat, Alberta. I've never been so cold, and we each separately thought we might actually die.

We didn't, and I don't remember anything else as we hitched our way across Saskatchewan prairies, Manitoba flatlands, then south down to Chicago, back up to Canada and Toronto – then got ready to leave for Europe.

It must have taken two weeks.

My girlfriend, Tep, was working at a women's camp up in northern Ontario – First Nations territory. I took a tiny pup tent up to be near her and spent two weeks in the fields.

The tent was so small that when I caught a case of poison oak (much worse than poison ivy) it covered every inch of my body – which swelled up like a balloon.

Miraculously, Tep escaped it. I was so swollen I couldn't stand up properly and had to walk all crunched up for several miles to reach the nearest First Nations village and a doctor.

We said goodbye to our girlfriends and families and flew to New York.

Neither of us had been in a plane before.

I was extremely excited, couldn't believe the whole thing. How could it possibly work? Thrust and lift versus weight and drag always amazes me.

I was zipping around, staring out windows at the world spinning below. The Old Masters never saw anything like this!

But Gray was quiet and 'adult', as if this was a perfectly normal experience and I was embarrassing him.

That night in New York I had the worst ever psychosomatic toothache, and unsuccessfully ran around the streets, failing to find oil of cloves or any other help. (Was this because you sensed you were leaving home for good, Dick?) Next day we got on an ancient green ship and the pain suddenly vanished, never to return. The ship was on its final voyage and, like most of its elderly women passengers, going home to Greece to die.

It was old and rough and we were in the cheap seats down in the hold, in a small room full of pipes.

Gray had a terrific sense of humour and we both were mimics. We had a mostly hilarious time down there acting out the voices and clichés in all the Hollywood movies – epics, Westerns and melodramas. We managed all the parts. Early in the morning I would come up with an accurate Vincent Price and Gray did a terrific Sir Felix Aylmer (who always played the King of England): 'This is the first time I take the hand of a Saxon.' Then we would fall around helplessly.

How could I have any idea that I would later be able to hire both these actors as voices for characters in my film work?

We also did a lot of drawings of fellow passengers.

Our first sight of land and first sight of Europe was on a sunny day as dolphins raced, leaped and played alongside the ship's prow. In front of us was ancient (and modern) Lisbon, perched on top of the Portuguese hills.

'Oh man, this is for me!'

We got off our old tub at Barcelona, then caught a ferry to Majorca and another ferry to the small island of Ibiza. Ibiza was a miracle. An ancient semi-Babylonian island. We both fell in love with it. It was like nothing we'd ever seen.

A LITTLE ISLAND

Graham didn't stay long. He wanted to get back to Canada, and gave up the plan to visit Europe's art galleries. I said, You're all set, you're gonna go home and be famous, and he did, and that's what quite quickly happened. He became tremendously successful.

Ibiza

I had the opportunity to be in this completely different culture. I was free, I had money for a year, this wonderful opportunity just to think, and read, and paint – I thought maybe there was an alternative life I could lead. But I had practically nothing to read, and so I sent away to the British Consulate for some books, and got back ones on yoga and, funnily enough, Karel Reisz's book on film editing, which I found interesting.

There were practically no people like me on Ibiza then. I started playing a lot of trumpet, 'cos I was alone, quiet, and the neighbours didn't mind. It was a wonderful life because the island was a Babylonian kind of place, so I was able to rethink, to start again.

It was an amazing time. I was calmer than I'd ever been because I didn't have any worries. I was shedding a lot of conditioning. I was feeling brave. I thought I'd be living there forever. And then I got an idea for a film. It just snuck up on me.

I was doing these very realistic paintings – dark brown. I did a big painting of Pepe's bar, where I played the cornet. There were six figures – some fishermen, Pepe, and me in the corner. Occasionally, I'd think of animation.

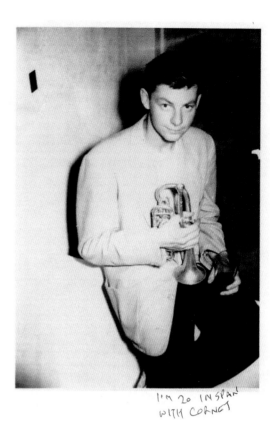

'I'm 20 in Spain with cornet'

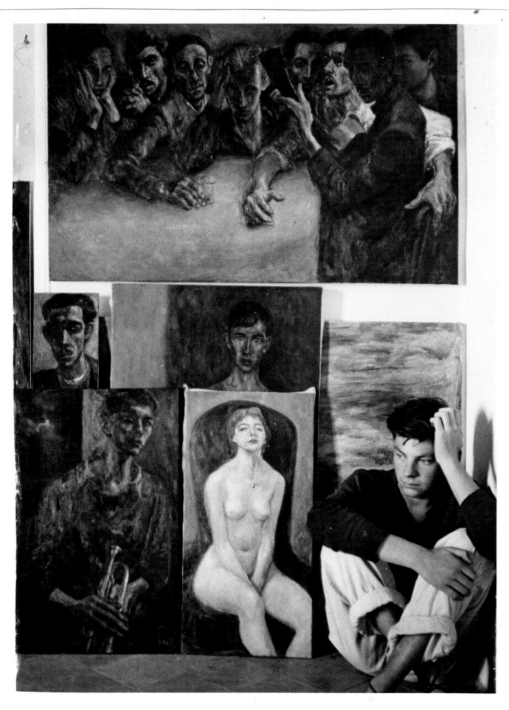

With Ibizan paintings including of Pepe's bar

I had a German friend who fancied himself as a philosopher. He had theories about people stuck in their different cultures. I noticed that when people would argue on the beach, they had fixed points of view. We all had these set ideals – like goodness, truth and beauty. And, gradually, this idea snuck into the back of my head.

I noticed that my pictures were trying to move. There was this painting that had a double exposure – my best painting so far. There were these children flying, everything was trying to move. I'd always been terribly impressed by Degas who said, 'I'm not a painter of dancers, I'm a painter of movement.' And movement is a very big thing for me.

Frank Herrmann, who was a friend of mine, took a photo of me, sitting double-exposed in front of this painting, like I'm thinking of it. Frank visited the island as an English photography student. We became friends and he took all kinds of pictures of me; he chronicled my studio. The photo of me jumping on the cover of this book is a shot by Frank.

There was a German architect living on Ibiza called Erwin Broner, who was now retired. He had worked as an animator on George Pál's puppetoons in the 1940s and 50s, using hand puppets, which moved frame by frame. I showed him storyboard stuff, which became the basis for *The Little Island*. He was able to help me enormously. He'd say, 'This is how you break it into sequences'; then we'd time it – we got a stopwatch – and we'd run through it. He'd force me to be very accurate. I put the thing together over three or four months. I had it all over the walls of my place.

Later, when I came back to England, we made a film together for Ford cars – Karel Reisz was the producer. I designed it with these very crazy cartoons of Erwin's – and they were startling.

Becoming involved in animation again was the turning point of my life. I realised that as an art form it was absolutely on the cutting edge of my culture, even if it didn't have the prestige of fine art. I thought: I'm gonna take it and make it carry more information, make it deal with different things.

It was a medium I could do something with, a product of today that I could take where other people hadn't gone. It was fresh – suddenly I wasn't trying to produce the dark paintings of the previous century. Somehow I had found the medium I wanted to be in. I'd already had a background in animation and cartoons, but then on Ibiza I'd veered off to painting. But now I came back to it.

Of course, I was very conscious that you can't get the depth into the animation that you can into a beautiful drawing or painting – but that's the

The Little Island **all over the walls**

challenge. I said okay, I'll take it as a challenge. And when I look at my most recent film *Prologue*, it does have some of that there, quite a bit anyway.

I got there a bit late, but I got there.

THE CONCEPTION OF *THE LITTLE ISLAND*

While I was on Ibiza, I noticed that people tended to come from a certain ideal – for instance, the Greeks talked about three: goodness, truth and beauty. I would be somebody who would go for beauty, but a socially responsible American travelling through Europe, a do-gooder, would be judging everything from the social aspect; goodness would be the main thing. But a scientist would be into the truth. This is a very crude division, but you could divide societies into what they prioritised to achieve their particular ideal.

So the idea was that the cartoon would show three guys arrive on an island, they go into their fantasies and then, of course, the fantasies start to collide, and they become monstrous in different ways – and I thought animation could show this. I'd never seen it done, but I was going do a philosophical film, without a single spoken word – and I wished I could leave out the words 'goodness' and 'truth' and 'beauty', but they'd be the only words used.

At that time expectation of a nuclear holocaust was the main issue, so one of the three guys, the scientist, creates the bomb, and the other two are at each other's throats in this mammoth fantasy where they change shape, but then it's left hanging at the end – they just zip back into their normal shapes, and leave the island.

As for the shape of the characters – I like Paul Klee, his things are very small, and looking at his work a lot took me away from the Disney or American cartoon structures. I was doing tiny storyboard drawings of these three little characters, and they weren't like Paul Klee, but he freed me. They were blobs really; very, very simple. I just plotted it out, gradually; I started drawing it very, very small, and then it got big. The thing just grew, and my interest in animation grew as well, because I thought: nobody's done a philosophical film, this could be quite a new thing.

So I was in this wonderful position that I'd never been in before: here I am, this young artist, I've got talent, what am I gonna do with my life? I can choose, I don't have to grind out crap. I knew how ignorant I was, but I also knew how smart I was. So I thought, what the hell, I'll take a run at this film, I know it's gonna be an awful lot of work.

My father gave me the addresses of three friends of his in Paris, where I was living for a few months. One of them was the Ethiopian ambassador to France, Imru Zelleke. We really hit it off, so I showed him my idea for the film. He thought it was terrific. He said, I will back, I will pay for it, and I said, you're crazy, how can you pay for this, this is gonna take a long time, but he said, I am paying for your film. Over time, his interest in the film grew, and the more I showed him of my storyboards, the more he thought it was terrific.

When Imru said he would back the film, I gave him my last painting from my time in Ibiza – three children on a swing; it was like a dream picture. It's the one where I have the double exposure. I gave the painting as a down payment to Imru because I figured it was my best painting, and that it could be worth money.

I planned to go to London, and contacted a small animation studio – Eddie Radage – who'd made Murray Mint commercials, and had advised me. They wouldn't hire me to do any work, but I thought I was going to have money anyway, because Imru was definite. He said he'd set up an account, so I said I was going to spend five hundred quid, the cost of getting the camera people. Suddenly Imru vanished. And I was out of money myself. So I never got what he had offered in return for my painting.

I suddenly had a five-hundred-quid loan from the bank – with no way to pay it off. So I wrote to my parents and said, I'm making a film, but I'm stuck for five hundred pounds to pay for it. And Mom wrote back and said, we can't do that. And my dad told her to tell me to stop.

Well, I started to earn my way out with bits of work on commercials. I also decided I'd have to have a film company, which I called Island Film Company. I can do lettering, so I produced an acceptable professional notepaper. I also thought I'd better do something about music for the film, so I went to the De Wolfe Music company because I thought, I can use known music. I went up to the door of their office, and there were signs for all these companies, including a very big one that said Island Film Company.

So I went in, and talked to the guy, who was very patronising, and it was like, 'Oh don't worry sonny, we'll help you.' I remember that tears welled up in my eyes and I couldn't see to get out. I went into the road and burst into tears. I thought, Oh God, I'm way out of my depth here.

There was a long period of struggle, doing bits and pieces of commercials for anybody. I got to know Bob Godfrey, who was an ex-commando, and he and another guy called Keith had a company called Biographic Cartoons – a very interesting, very funky, kind of half-arsed operation; they did anything they could get. Bob didn't have any money to pay me, or maybe just a bit every now and then, but he said, 'If you do our commercial art stuff, you can use our camera for your film.'

So I worked there for about nine months, so I could shoot tests on the camera, as well as trying to shoot finished things. Bob thought I was the hottest commercial artist he'd ever run into because I could do all the different stuff.

This was the beginning of a three-year battle. And I decided to do everything silent; I didn't go back to the De Wolfe Music company.

Eddie Radage, whose company I'd written to, was especially kind to me. He and his partner, Dave, looked at my storyboards and said this, that and the other, and suggested what I should do. I learned from them about exposure sheets. They'd say, use the action column – you draw the line of the action for a second. In the middle of all of this, I was painting the things myself; I'd trace and animate, but I couldn't afford the paint they used for animation. Disney had special paint for cels that nobody else had, though it wasn't any good as the paint popped off the cels.

A German-American painter, Karl Zerbe, had discovered a new medium

With cels from *The Little Island*

74

to paint with – polyvinyl acetate. It dries immediately. So I got a bottle of it. Polyvinyl acetate is what you use to paint walls. It has a plastic base, and I figured: hey, wait a minute, this will fit onto the plastic cels that we use. So I went to Dave and said, I'm sure this is going to work.

We slapped it on these cels, mixed with normal watercolour. Then we hit it with hammers. It didn't come off. Perfect! I thought: I've discovered the paint everybody needs to use! Nobody had this paint, and I said, I can make money, money to finance the film! Well, I tried to find a businessman who would recognise this, saying that this is going to be the paint everybody will use. But of course I couldn't get the scheme off the ground, how could I have done that?

Little Island **still**

However, I used it for the entire film, and then gradually the other studios started using it too. When I went to work at UPA's London studio, I took it with me. It took them ten years to realise what I'd discovered, and then they made a big business out of providing the world supply of that paint.

Sometime after I got to London, and was quite poor, and getting nowhere fast, somebody saw my storyboards for *The Little Island*, and said: 'You should go to Finch's pub where all the movie people go. Tristram Cary, who just did the soundtrack for *The Ladykillers*, drinks there.'

Cary was a pioneer in electronic music – especially *musique concrète* – and was on the cutting edge of contemporary sound; he'd been a radar engineer in the war. So I went along to Finch's and showed him my drawings, and he seemed quite taken by them. We met a couple of times and I went through everything with him. He knew I had nothing, no cash or anything. And he said, 'I'm going to do your film. First, I'm going to take it to my dad.'

And his dad turned out to be Joyce Cary. I couldn't believe it.

So, Tris took the drawings to his dad. I'd written a whole screenplay, but Joyce apparently said: forget the words, do more drawings. And over three and a half years Tris covered me – because I couldn't earn enough – by extending his mortgage. I paid him back at the end, for everything.

Cartoon of me and Tris on the film

I'd show bits of the film as I was making it. The first screening was at the National Film Theatre. Leslie Hardcastle, who was running it, would let me use the projection room every now and then, and people were very interested in what I was doing. The word got out that I was making something good. Of course, Tris gave it his seal of approval – this mattered as he was then one of the hottest film composers going. Sandy Mackendrick, whom he'd worked with on *The Ladykillers*, said I was a genius.

With Tris and the sound editor Francis Bieber in the cutting room

So, it was the absolute turning point.

Then, when I was about two years into making the film, UPA came to London. They'd had a very big success with the *Mr Magoo* films, and with their short films, including my favourite, *Rooty Toot Toot*. They had expanded from Hollywood, and had come to London to do commercials, which was a good idea – but they didn't have a director; they'd expanded without proper talent.

George Dunning was hired as the director. George was scared because he didn't have experience. And there was also a fellow called Leo Salkin, who looked exactly like Mr Magoo. He'd been a Disney story artist. I tried to get a job as an animator, and showed Leo some of my animation on *The Little Island*, but the images were too far out for him, so he didn't give me a job. This was at a time when I was really in trouble financially.

But then I said, 'Look, you need paint for this stuff, right? You're going to set up a trace department. Well, I've discovered this animation paint, so I can mix it, and do the trace and paint.' He said, 'Okay.' And when I showed it to him, he said, 'Wow, this is the stuff!' And that's how the paint started getting into the industry.

When you have three or four levels of cels, with maybe a head on one, and feet on the other, and something else on another, you want it all to merge as the same colour. So I mixed up all the paint, and did the trace and paint. I had money coming in, as an actual regular thing, and this helped me finish *The Little Island*.

Cel from *The Little Island*

This lasted for about three or four months. Then I did a commercial for Bob Godfrey with a television screen that was curved like a head. I drew two eyes on it, and a nose and a big mouth. I had the character smile and lick his lips. I just had a piece of cardboard and ran a cardboard tongue around it. It was crude. I did it for peanuts.

Leo Salkin came in one day, and said: 'You did this commercial? You animated that?' And I said, 'Yes.' 'Well then,' he said, 'you're an animator.' He had rejected *The Little Island*, which was far more sophisticated. But the commercial had a strong graphic idea. UPA's whole *raison d'être* was strong graphics. It wasn't Disney. It wasn't smooth. It hit you in your face.

So suddenly I was an animator! And six months later, I was directing – because nobody knew what they were doing. Now I was the hot shot! And my reputation was becoming international; people like Corny Cole heard about me, and said, 'There's a guy in London who's really good.' Suddenly everything changed. So when *The Little Island* came out, I was known, I was a character.

In the studio with a *Little Island* poster

The response to the film was amazement – because there'd been nothing like it. All the intelligentsia went wild. Imagine, the first ever philosophic animated film. It was about the state of the world, metaphorically. A hell of a lot of metaphors. I was accepted into the cultural scene along with Lindsay Anderson and Karel Reisz; David Robinson wrote a marvellous piece about me in *The Times*. I wasn't the toast of the town, but I was recognised as somebody of real interest – a lone worker who had made it to the top. The film won a big prize at the Venice Biennale, and caused a ruckus in the animation world.

However, I couldn't get a distributor.

DUBBED "THE LITTLE ISLAND" JANUARY 24 1958

SEQUENCE	ROUGH TIME	DESCRIPTION	MUSIC COMPOSED	RECORDED	PLANNED AND DOPE-SHEETED	COLOUR and LAYOUT	BACK-GROUNDS PAINTED	AN.
Titles AND CREDITS	50 sec	Credits Then Little MEN						
Sequence (1)	24 sec	Universe down to Sun	RANK SAID YES					
Sequence (2)	97 sec	Sun to island — men's arrival, sun-burning (to time-passing)	WON 1ST PRIZE VE EXPERIMENTAL					
Sequence (3)	123 sec	Urk. Discussion (time-passing)	SHORTS AND DOCUMENTARY film festival JULY 24					
Sequence (4A)	88 sec	Yoga TRUTH Vision (and reaction)	NOMINATED for BAFTA					
Sequence (4B)	315 sec	Aesthetic BEAUTY Vision (and reaction)	OPENED at CURZON CINEMA					
Sequence (4C)	140 sec	Social GOOD Vision (and reaction) (TIME-PASSING)	WON BRITISH FILM Best Animated Film					
Sequence (5A)	60 sec	First provocation	MARCH 18, 1959					
Sequence (5B)	116 sec	Second provocation (and small) battle	WON HONORABLE MENTION					
Sequence (5C)	300 seconds	Third + biggest provocation to huge fight up to film CLIMAX						
Sequence (6)	55 sec	pull-out men dress-leave-beating holds up to universe + end						
CINEMASCOPE SECTION	SAME AS 5c.	DONE						

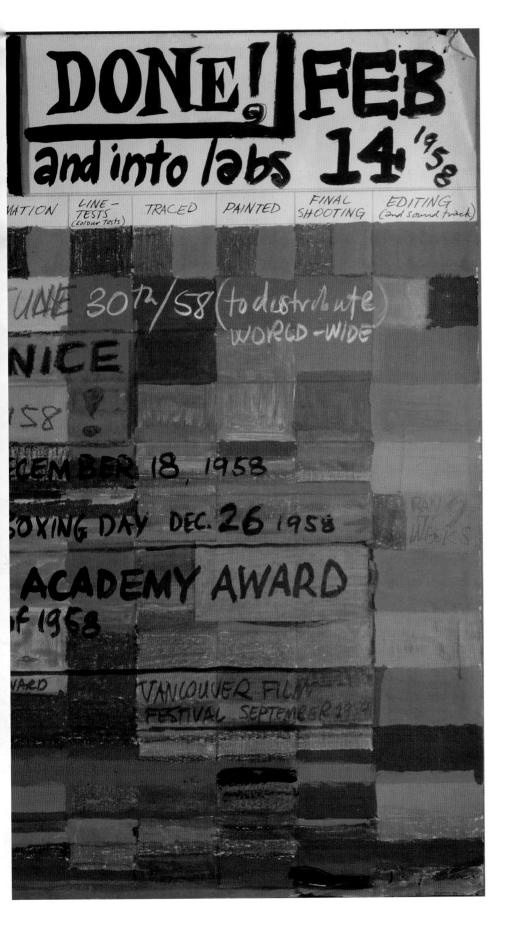

Little Island schedule

DICK HUEMER: 'ATTENTION TO DETAIL'

With Dick Huemer

I was 25, broke, in debt and exhausted from the three and a half years' effort to make my first film, *The Little Island* – a half-hour allegorical, philosophic satire on idealists, with no spoken words. It won a lot of international awards but only had a very limited art-house release; it was not your usual commercial fare. I gave myself ten out of ten for effort and tenacity but only three out of ten for my ability to realise my conception. This was in 1958.

A year later I got a really encouraging letter from someone at Disney's called Dick Huemer, along with a book of poetry, *A Dragon on the Hill Road* by Richard Huemer. It was inscribed:

RICHARD WILLIAMS –

FOR HAVING PRODUCED

THE FIRST TRULY POETIC

ANIMATED CARTOON – MY

SINCEREST CONGRATULATIONS

Dick

Huemer

11/11/59

I almost fell over as I realised this was from the guy who was (with Joe Grant) the story director on *Dumbo* – my favourite, along with *Snow White*!

I couldn't believe it. I still can't see the sense in it, but that's how Dick felt. It was not hard to see that we'd become friends. I got a lot of encouragement from this man, which makes a hell of a lot of difference when you're out on your own.

Dick was born in New York City in 1898. He was born eight years after his compatriot Grim Natwick, who said about him: 'Dick was one of the artists who helped build the early framework of animation. He was with animation through all its growing pains. Whatever animation became, he helped to shape it, drawing by drawing, idea by idea.'

In 1916, when Dick was 18, he studied for a year at the Art Students League of New York. He saw a sign on a doorway near his Bronx home, 'Raoul Barré, Cartoonist'. He said, 'I walked up the stairs and I walked into the animating business.'

He began his long career animating silent *Mutt and Jeff* shorts at the Barré-Bowers Studio. From 1916 until 1930 he worked in New York, then went west, and in 1933 joined the Disney studio and spent the rest of his life as a key player there. He was a living, walking history of the medium from its beginnings through to the fruition of its golden age and well beyond.

Dick could draw. When he went to work for Max Fleischer at his leading New York studio, he became one of the top men in the field, maybe *the* top man. He certainly was the most famous animator – known for his unsurpassed animation for *Koko the Clown*.

Dick told me that in 1930:

Roy Disney kept taking me out to dinner in New York and trying to hire me to join them in LA. But Polly [Dick's wife] and I loved the east – opera, fine art, the culture, gourmet food and all that – and just didn't want to move west.

But *one* thing kept bothering me – I kept seeing these Disney cartoons and they just kept getting better and better. And *better*! They were getting *so* good that I started to think that Walt had a secret weapon – a special secret. Now I was a top man and I knew there couldn't *be* a secret to it. I knew it was crazy, but I kept thinking there must be a secret.

But when I did finally go to Disney's, I found out what the secret was! There *was* one!

'What was it?' I panted.

Dick said, 'It was *"attention to detail"* – that was the secret.'

I remember flying back to London after this conversation and rushing into my studio with the news. I said to our receptionist, 'Quick – I've got the secret of animation! Type out a memo to everyone in the studio!' I dictated all that Dick had told me, that the secret was – attention to detail – which is borne out by our own experience in anything decent that we've done so far – *Attention to detail*!

The memo went out and arrived on my desk. It contained fourteen typos.

Dick and Polly finally did move west – but not to work with Walt Disney. Dick had accepted a lucrative offer to direct at Charles Mintz's studio. But he regretted turning down Walt's offer the minute he did so. Dick told writer Joe Adamson: 'Walt was such a thundering success that I bitterly regretted I had turned him down and gone with Mintz and just frittered away three years on making good money but doing little else that I could be proud of.'

Dick couldn't help admiring Walt's superior stuff and wanting to be a part of it, so when the Great Depression forced Mintz to cut salaries and his staff went on strike, Dick got a friend at Disney's to let Walt know that he wanted to work for him now. That was it, but Dick had to take less than half the money he had been making. But he was happy about it and was astonished at Walt himself. 'One couldn't help feeling awe in the presence of genius. We all felt we were in on something historic.' He also discovered that he had to work like hell just to keep up with the level of work being turned out by the powerful new animators at the studio.

By 1938, after many *Silly Symphonies* and animating a section of *Snow White* – the bed-building sequence which was cut out of the picture because it held up the story – Dick was 40 years old. He'd been a leading animator for twenty years and he just couldn't stand it any more. He told me, 'You know, I was just too lazy to keep animating. You have to work too hard. I was happy in story.' He went to Walt and said he'd really had it, couldn't stand to even walk a figure across a page any more – was there an opening for a director? There was, and Dick absolutely loved it. Then he gradually, and logically, moved into story development.

Dick says Walt always introduced him with, 'Meet Dick Huemer – he goes to operas.' Dick had also studied violin, and was passionate about classical music, and wrote poetry. He said that's why he got on *Fantasia* and became the story director (with Joe Grant) on that film.

Though he was relaxed and easy-going, Dick had a tough mind in – as he would say – a lazy way. He was an urbane, sophisticated and well-read fellow with a strong sense of storytelling. He loved Disney's. He told me, 'The Disney studio was like a country club for us – I *loved* to go to work.'

Dick also told me:

Walt wasn't interested in money per se. He really *wasn't*. It was only fuel to him. One thing people nowadays don't realise is that when we were making the great films, the studio was always in financial trouble! I remember them telling us – 'We're going to make *Cinderella* now and if it isn't a hit, we're out of business. It'll be the last one.' It wasn't until after Disneyland got going that there was lots of money around here.

Walt was great with us main guys. Even gave us share options – but he was bitterly disappointed in us when we sold our Disney shares and bought other stuff. I was one of them – sold Disney and bought Lockheed. What a mistake! Walt was very disappointed in us that we didn't have enough faith in the studio.

As he grew older, Dick kept working in and out of the studio. He did the script for the Academy Award winner *Toot, Whistle, Plunk and Boom* (1953), worked on television shows and, towards the end, wrote Disney's *True Life Adventures* comic strip. My impression was that he was a happy, fulfilled man. His three boys had grown up – one a doctor, one a successful businessman, and the youngest an anthropologist who became a fully-fledged member of a Plains Indian tribe. Dick lived with his wife, Polly, in a large *Snow White*-like house under giant evergreens in the residential section of old Burbank, just around the corner from the studio.

He'd had heart trouble and did long walks and became prohibited from eating the food he'd loved. He said to me once, when some of us were ramming down a big breakfast, 'You know I was always this big gourmet, don't you?' 'Yes.' 'And you know what it is that I miss *most* of all?' 'No.' 'Bacon and eggs.' So much for a lifetime of gourmet-ism!

Dick was always cheering me on. Here's a sample:

> I enjoyed your treatment of *Christmas Carol* very much, as I do almost everything you have done. Make that: I DO enjoy everything you have done. So just keep a-doing it.

> The fantasy parts of your show thrilled me to the bone. I mean, really gave me goose pimples. I hope it was nice and remunerative.

Here's a page of things I typed out years ago that Dick had told me.

> All Disney ever wanted was to entertain – with excellence.

> He said, 'We'll make it so good they'll have to want it.'

> Disney was the first to worry about the audience – about the fellow who paid his twenty-five cents or fifty cents to get in. Before that, we used to just make private jokes, what we thought was funny. But Disney would say – Are *they* with us? Do *they* follow the story? Do *they* understand what is happening? Get the entertainment right.

> Walt never said when he liked a thing – but you knew he liked it if he did.

> He was the first one to think about *weight* in cartoons.

> Walt was never with you. He was single-minded. He would always be thinking how to make it better.

> He had a fantastic memory for everything.

> Walt had such a good memory he could put his hand in and pull out any gag to fit any situation. He analysed everything. Seldom laughed, except at his own jokes.

> I always hated going to meetings with Walt. He was such an unpleasant bastard. He put the hair up on the back of your neck. But you always knew he was trying to make a job better.

> Walt never thought about art or aesthetics. Later on he did but, at first, all he ever thought of was getting the entertainment right.

Walt always needed an audience. Kids, anybody, anywhere. He was a son of a bitch. Then he'd find an audience, then *click* into his act and then *click* out of it.

In 1916 animators already said, 'If people can do it – don't do it.' Here at the Studio things have never been so prosperous what with the smashing success of the Florida-based dollars that are reaped every time one of the old pictures is re-released. *Song of the South* is just knocking 'em dead at the box office all over the country. As you will remember, this picture contains some of our best animation – the Uncle Remus segments with Br'er Fox etc.

Dick gave me strong advice on some of my own work:

'I miss the clean, hard-cut line. Simplicity is art. One reason you like *Dumbo* is that it has a straight line right through – from start to finish.'

And: 'Where do you break people's hearts?'

Dick died of heart failure in 1979. He was 81. He died in the hospital right across the street from the studio.

LOVE ME, LOVE ME, LOVE ME

My second film was an eight-minute short called *Love Me, Love Me, Love Me*, and it was meant to be my goodbye to animation. I thought, I'll make this, nobody else is ever going to think this is funny, but I think it's funny. I'll make this and I'll quit and I'll go back to paint in the Mediterranean.

The idea came from a friend, Stan Hayward. He was a merchant seaman, and a writer as well. He came back from a trip to Singapore and showed me a sick bag from his flight. He said, 'I was chatting up the air hostess, and I wrote this silly thing about this Squidgy Bod character.' I read it and thought, that's a really funny idea there. I'd seen Kenneth Williams in a film, *Carry On Doctor*, and he had this crazy voice that I thought was perfect for this Squidgy Bod.

Once upon a time, there lived a man called Squidgy Bod. Everybody loved him though everything he did was wrong; but still, little children would follow him, horses would wave their tails at him. But there also lived a man (we didn't have a name for him yet) who did everything right, but everybody hated him, especially children. So this guy took a course on being loved.

I thought it was a terrific idea, and I decided to make it to show my two sides: Dick the cartoonist and Dick the artist.

I got Kenneth to do it. I went to where they were shooting another *Carry On* film and managed to get through to him. I said to Kenneth, 'I must have your voice for this crazy film. It's dependent on you because of the innuendo.'

I showed him some drawings and said, 'If you don't do it, I won't do it, because it's not going to work unless it's you' – which was true.

He said, 'I'll do it.' He did it in one take!

He did it for practically nothing; he was very pleased, he thought it was a classic masterpiece.

I remember going to the first screening on Oxford Street thinking it was just a private joke. But the audience fell around laughing at the exact same things I thought were funny. British Lion tested it out, and it was a huge success. They sent it round the world with whatever films they were releasing, like the Boulting Brothers' films. It got reviewed in *Playboy*, who said: You have to go and see this crazy, whimsical Englishman's short. So it went around the world again and guess what came through the door? Cheques! My God, there was a market for my work.

With Kenneth Williams

However, there was a complication – I was in debt to the tax man. Luckily my friend the film producer Anthony Perry had one of those mathematical minds, and he said, I think you've been double-taxed. If you earned one hundred quid, put ninety into the film, and lived on ten, they're charging you double somehow.

Squidgy Bod with the little children

He took it to the tax man and after a while they agreed: Yes, you've been over-taxed by five thousand pounds. However, as you're a foreigner, we're not going to pay it back to you, unless you stay in this country for five years. Then you can have your money.

So, with the success of *Love Me, Love Me, Love Me*, and the thought that in five years I'd have five thousand pounds, I stayed. And that is the reason why I didn't leave England, and why I started a studio and ended up in animation.

WHAT'S NEW PUSSYCAT?

Now I knew I had a commercial voice – I had all kinds of stuff going on, like storyboarding *Yellow Submarine*. So I got to thinking that maybe I should start taking animation seriously, maybe make a bigger picture.

In the middle of all this, the *Observer* did a big article about me – many pages, including the cover of the magazine section. As a result, I got to do the titles on *What's New Pussycat?*. I stole one of George Dunning's office boys, a kid called Charlie Jenkins. Charlie knew about photography, which I didn't. He figured a way in which we could use light from behind the drawings – cut through the drawings so that we'd get a spray of light, and you could control it.

The director was Clive Donner. He had just directed his first high-profile feature, which was Harold Pinter's *The Caretaker*. It had great prestige. So they got Clive to direct this crazy film with a screenplay by Woody Allen (his first) about a womaniser, played by Peter O'Toole, and a bunch of women. The film was loopy, but it got a lot of attention and made a lot of money. *What's New Pussycat?* was a big hit. Woody Allen was in it, Burt Bacharach did the music, and Tom Jones sang the title song.

I actually had something to do with the music, because I wanted the titles to come in like the old days, when you went to the movies and they had slides for tobacco ads. So I wanted to slide in the artwork, like a trombone slide.

The titles came in like stills, but I had them back-lit, because of Charlie's cleverness. It was art nouveau, which always looks terrific on a black background.

So I asked Burt – as the titles slid in – 'Can you write me a Dixieland trombone slide, sort of brrrr umpty da?' and he did – it goes, 'brrrrrruum, What's new pussycat? Whoa, whoa, whoa!'

So *What's New Pussycat?* was a big success.

With Ursula Andress on set

COMMERCIALS

A few years earlier I had been at a party where I said to Clive Donner, 'Clive, you spent years at J. Walter Thompson making black and white commercials. Those must have been horrendous years; it must have driven you crazy doing baby food ads.'

And he said, 'No, not really.'

I said, 'Oh come on, it's just crap. When I do these things, I just knock 'em out, take the cash.'

Now Clive was quite a mild guy, but he stood me up against the wall, and said, 'You're wrong! You should be giving everything you do your best. I learned a lot of the stuff I needed to know in order to shoot a feature film dealing with babies, who are very difficult. That's how I learned my craft.'

I said, 'Yeah, but it took so long', and he said, 'Look, why don't you, for the first time, take the next commercial, whatever it is, for big baby napkins – or any damn thing – and give it your absolute best. Just do it as an experiment, see what happens.'

So I said, 'Okay, I will.' I was very lucky. A good idea came in for a commercial for Guinness – Guinness at the Albert Hall! There was a choir of large women, and a little German conductor came in, and they sang. We had a big ensemble, and it was in colour because it was for the movies. And I gave it my very best shot. The damn thing won ten awards!

Super Softies
Tempest
Gold Margarine
Cresta Elvis

91

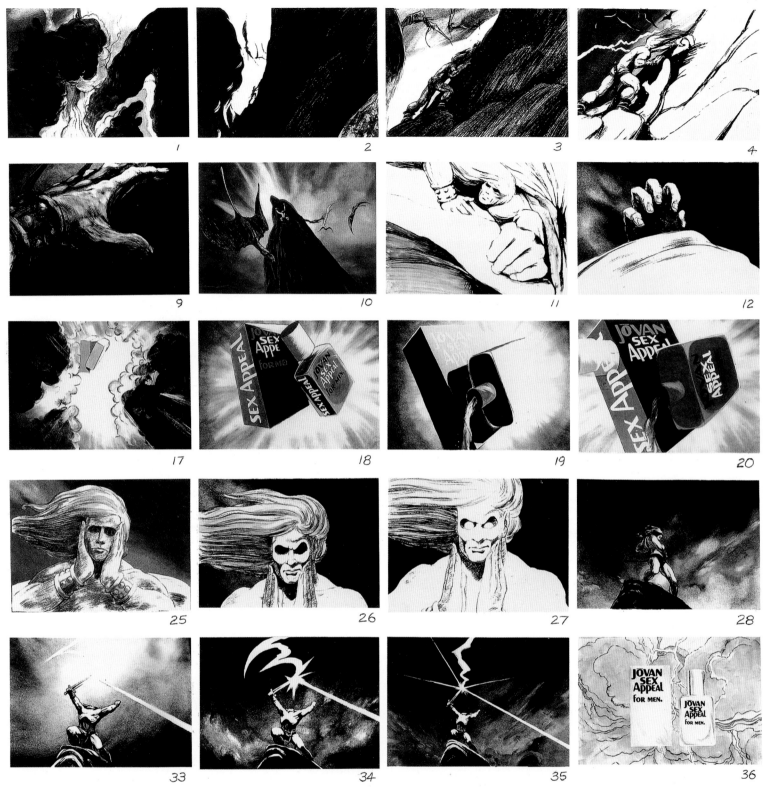

HERE'S A COMMERCIAL JOB THAT I'M NOT ASHAMED OF. THIS WAS BASED ON A FRANK FRAZETTA POSTER THAT the J.WALTER THOMPSON AD AGENCY PAID TO USE. AS FAR AS I KNOW, THIS WAS the FIRST T.V. AD TO SELL MALE PERFUME—HENCE the OVERSTATED MACHO APPROACH— i.e."REAL" MEN WEAR PERFUME. THIS WAS IN 1978-the FIRST JOB FOR MY LITTLE HOLLYWOOD STUDIO. USUALLY WE'D GET 3 MONTHS TO MAKE A 30-SECOND ADVERT. FOR SOME REASON THERE WERE ONLY 6 WEEKS TO DO IT. EXCEPT FOR the SKY, BACKGROUNDS, the PACK and PAINTING

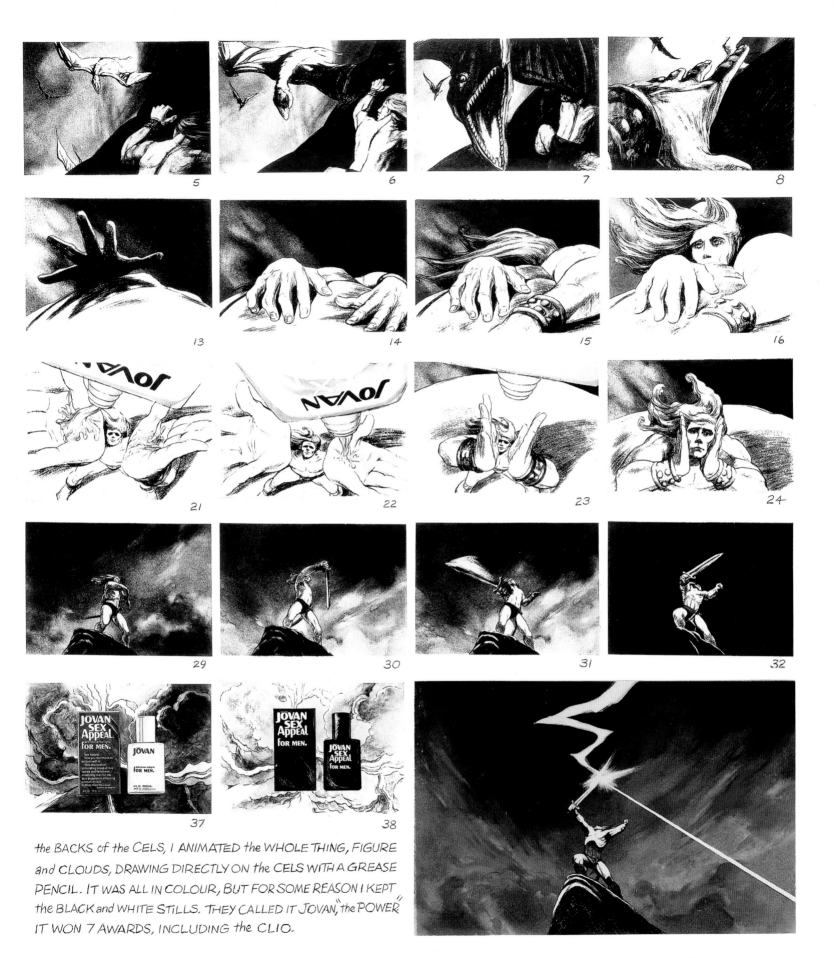

the BACKS of the CELS, I ANIMATED the WHOLE THING, FIGURE and CLOUDS, DRAWING DIRECTLY ON the CELS WITH A GREASE PENCIL. IT WAS ALL IN COLOUR, BUT FOR SOME REASON I KEPT the BLACK and WHITE STILLS. THEY CALLED IT JOVAN," the POWER" IT WON 7 AWARDS, INCLUDING the CLIO.

THE CHARGE OF THE LIGHT BRIGADE

I had quite a successful studio going and then I got a tremendous break. The director Tony Richardson, who was a very brave man, hired me to do ten minutes of his epic film *The Charge of the Light Brigade.* I was to animate in the style of 1850s illustration – like the *Illustrated London News* and *Punch* magazine – so everything was crosshatched engravings.

I was actually quite proud of it. I thought – we've really succeeded – we used these little dissolves; it was pioneering. Nobody had done anything like it or, if they had, it hadn't worked. As we were finishing, Ken Harris – who was the best Warner Bros. animator – started working with us. He came to the studio and we ran this thing for him in the theatre in the week of the premiere.

At the end of it all, we leaned forward and said, 'What do you think, Ken?' and Ken said, 'Wow, you know, you guys, I don't know how you did all that crosshatching, all that work, all those drawings,' and then he said, 'But it don't move too good.'

It was like a right smack to the jaw, but I thought, yeah, he's right, I gotta really start the serious study of movement.

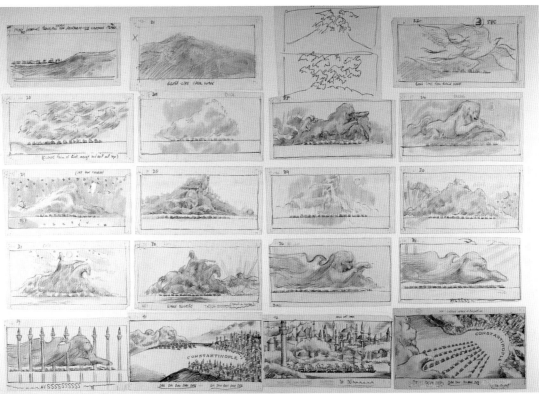

Queen and country shout 'War' cel
Fleet travels to Sebastopol storyboard

Fall of Sebastopol storyboard

KEN HARRIS: 'PUT EVERYTHING IN THE RIGHT PLACE'

I first met Ken at a London hotel as the elevator doors opened. I inadvertently started laughing. 'I know,' he smiled, 'I look like the coyote.'

Ken was 69 years old then and he really *did* change my life. His heart condition, which gave him angina, meant that he had to learn to suffer fools gladly. We gladly provided the fools. He was kind, but honest.

A year earlier, I was having dinner in London with Chuck Jones and I told him that since I was a little boy I could always spot Ken Harris's scenes in Chuck's cartoons. 'Impossible,' said Chuck, 'how could you?' 'Because his drawings have little square bits on them, very distinctive, very funny.' I then rattled off a whole bunch of scenes that Ken did and Chuck was astonished. 'You're right,' he said, 'unbelievable! Look, he's just retired – why don't you write him a fan letter? He might visit – his new wife is a traveller.'

So I wrote Ken a fan letter and back came a letter about English cars. I know nothing about cars but Ken and his wife, Kathy, came to England. We hit it off right away and Ken's retirement ended. We worked together for thirteen years till he was 82, when he just couldn't draw any more. I told him, 'I'll take blurs.'

When we started working together – he was 69, I was 37 – my real animation education began. Ken said in an interview, 'I was having a crack at retirement, putting up my legs, and it wasn't working very well. I was bored – wanting to get back to some work. When Dick asked me over, I jumped at the chance.'

Ken's real name was Karyl. He was born in 1898. His parents were farmers and moved with baby Ken in a covered wagon from California to Oregon. When Ken was 3, they moved to Washington State.

Ken said:

I remember when I was 5 years old (about 1904) my dad took me into a saloon where they had a thing where you looked into a viewer and you put in a nickel, and that automatically turned the light on, and you turned this crank, and the mechanism flipped a bunch of photographs. They had a file of photographs on a circular thing, you could get a real good picture if you turned it right. You could make any speed you wanted, too. It was all about 'The Doctor's Dilemma'. A doctor goes in to feel this woman's pulse, and the doctor takes her stockings off and all that. And if you came to a good sexy position, you could slow it down.

To me, at 5 years old, it was a big thing because it was the first time I saw pictures move. In that little town where we lived, they did not have movies. However, a year or so later our little town showed a movie in the church, of an old lady that dumped a load of children in a flour barrel. And that was the first movie I saw.

Ken was always crazy about cars. He'd owned 114 different ones. He had a passion for driving racing cars and was naturally mechanical. He got a job as a mechanical assistant with Pontiac

Young Ken and his first wife, Alta

and made it to assistant service manager but was laid off in the Great Depression. He turned to selling cars on his own, using the contacts he'd made at Pontiac.

By now Ken was happily married and in his early 30s. He started drawing cartoons for the sports and automobile pages of the *Los Angeles Examiner*. He loved doing it but they paid him practically nothing, so he kept on selling cars to survive.

He told me his mom read in the papers that animators in the Hollywood studios were making big money and she said, 'Why don't you try it, Ken? You do all those sports cartoons – maybe you can do it.'

Ken was lucky and became friendly with Webb Smith who was a top story man for Walt Disney. (Webb is credited by many with having invented the storyboard.) Webb encouraged Ken and helped him with contacts.

Ken said:

I didn't start animating until I was 35, that is, in 1934. I joined Boyd La Vero's studios. They were making a picture at the time I joined them. They had good business ideas: you could learn animation there but you had to pay them five dollars a week for the privilege. After about a week of being there, the boss came round and said he had been talking to his associates and they had noticed I had quite a flair for the job and was doing pretty well – and that next week I could work for nothing!

About a month later they started paying me about a dollar a foot but, in fact, I never got my money, as the film never got released. I stayed there about one year and learned a lot in a short time.

Then I went to Warner Bros., earning twelve dollars a week. We were working on *Merrie Melodies*, *Looney Tunes* and Daffy Duck. By that time I was really sold on animation. Webb Smith, who I'd kept in contact with, said I had a knack for action drawings; I always found that they came easily to me.

I spent six months as an in-betweener, then graduated to assistant for Bob McKimson. I don't know how you get to be an animator without being an assistant first. Usually, it took about five to ten years to become an animator unless you were a very adaptable guy. I was an assistant in-betweener and then the assistant animator, but I worked nights and animated. I probably did about 400 or 500 feet of animation in that year and a half. Some of it they used and some they didn't. But I was no kid, I was married and had to make a living. I couldn't horse around like the young guys did. They'd just go into it and say, 'Well, I'm working here in this studio and some day I'll be an animator.' They didn't seem to care about how quick, and they didn't seem to worry too much about it.

I was an assistant for just six months, but then I'd had experience from my cartoon drawings of sports – like baseball players – which helped me get to grips with action. I knew what to do with a foot, arm or whatever for the movement to look right. I knew where to put it, but I just couldn't draw real good.

Ken joined Chuck Jones's unit in 1937. He quickly became one of the lead animators working on Bugs Bunny, Porky Pig, Daffy Duck, etc. and, eventually, Wile E. Coyote and the Roadrunner.

Ken said, 'It was funny how Bugs Bunny came to be born. One of the guys at the studio was called Bugs Hardaway and he was dabbling around with a drawing of a rabbit. When we were looking for a new character, someone said, "Let's use Bugs' bunny." We did and the name stuck.'

Ken's stature at Warner Bros. kept rising. Chuck Jones certainly regarded him as his lead animator. I asked Ken why he never went over to work at Disney's. He said it was because he always felt a little unsure about his drawing. 'But I probably would have done well on a character like Goofy.' Also, Ken was very respected at Warner Bros. at a time when Bugs Bunny and Warner cartoons were more popular with the public than the Disney shorts. (Disney's top men only worked on their short cartoons in lulls between features, and the public was responding more to the wilder, more anarchic Warner shorts.)

My impression was that Ken was happily employed and valued at Warner Bros. – coming in early in the morning and working like hell producing lots and lots of excellent, funny footage, then going off to play tennis in the late afternoon.

Later on, Ken worked with Hanna-Barbera on Yogi Bear, then re-joined Chuck Jones's unit, now at MGM, working on the *Tom and Jerry* series. In 1966 he retired, and that's when Chuck suggested I write to him.

'There, there, old boy – help this young fellow out.'

Here's Ken being visited at my studio by his old boss, Chuck Jones. We were working on Dickens's *A Christmas Carol* and boy, did Ken ever help us out! Chuck got us the job and was the executive producer. He was great. We only saw him twice. *And* he lent us his men – Abe Levitow, Hal Ambro and George Nicholas – to help at the end.

Ken was used to Chuck Jones doing a lot of preliminary drawings for him, and I did it too. When we started, Ken said 'Gee, Dick, if I could draw like you, animation would be *fun*!' I shot back, 'Yeah, Ken, and if I could *animate* like you, animation would be fun!'

This old guy would arrive in London, sick with angina, looking like he might die at any minute, but as soon as he started to work, a magical transformation would occur. Within a week, sometimes in just a day or two, he would shed ten or fifteen years and become sharp, lithe and vital. He'd be the first one into our studio at 7.30 a.m., opening up the place, and work like mad until noon. Then he'd relax at lunch, coast until about 3 p.m., then go home and watch tennis on TV. And he'd *think* about the next day's work. He produced thirty or forty feet a week this way – three or four times what we did – and of course it was much better than ours.

When Art Babbitt arrived at our studio he had this 'living legend' aspect to him – the aristocratic demeanour of a celebrated exponent of the superior Disney tradition of excellence etc. – however friendly. Art knew Ken was very good. But almost every day after the rushes were shown and everybody had gone, Art would come quietly up to me and ask in a low voice, 'Who did *that* stuff?' I'd always say, 'Ken, you know, it's all his.'

'Oh,' he'd say, until the next day. Ken would be producing all this great work and it really shocked Art. He'd mutter, 'God, this guy Ken, where the hell did *he* come from?'

Ken would say to me, 'Gee, I wish I could work slow like Art. Maybe it would be better, but after all these years of having to bat out the footage, I don't think I *can* work slow. I wish I could.'

Flipping animation with Ken

102

Ken had great humour, though it wasn't immediately apparent. He had this wonderful knack – or flair – for something personal in his work that nobody else could get. Top animator and director Abe Levitow was trained by Ken. While working with us on *A Christmas Carol*, Abe, who was also 'fast and good', said, 'The old bastard, he's just got this incredible knack for movement and acting. And he's master of the charts. He's really kind of a lazy animator – because he's such a master of timing those charts that he can do the minimum amount of work and still get a great result.'

Ken told me they had to produce thirty feet a week on Bugs Bunny or be fired, so he would do forty feet and put ten feet under his desk, declare thirty and go off mid-afternoon to play tennis. But he sure wasn't lazy when he worked! He absolutely *hated* any interruptions. I had to have his paper ready for him, stacked sharp and edges crisp like a Bible and pencils sharp and vertically placed and – *no mess*! Only the job at hand – nothing else.

Ken was well known as a terrific athlete who hardly moved – very, very efficient and deliberate in his moves. The right thing at the right time done with simple efficiency – just like his animation. He was a champion dancer, a pool shark, a tennis whiz and a qualified international tennis umpire. He was socially pleasant but nobody's fool, and I think that any grumpiness resulted from his terrific concentration on the job at hand.

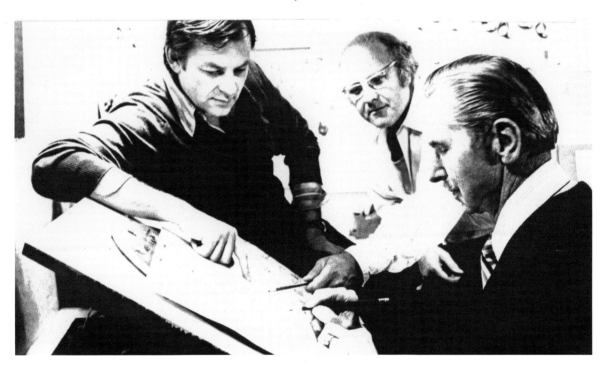

With Roy and Ken: me lurking as designer-layout man Roy Naisbitt works with Ken.
A good pool player, Roy was constantly whipped by pool shark Ken.

Every now and then, at least once a year, we'd be going down the street and Ken, with his bad heart condition, would suddenly sit down, white as a ghost and say, 'I think this is it.' Then after a few minutes he'd be okay again. This went on for over ten years.

Ken was about 77 and in delicate shape. One day we were crossing the street in Soho Square and we suddenly had to dodge a fast car. Ken leaped forward and snapped into an *exact* Warner Bros. cartoon run. I broke out laughing, but he didn't see what was funny. I'd seen that characteristic run of his in thirty years of cartoons!

Caricature of Ken running

I said to him, 'Early on, when I traced off your work, I learned an enormous amount and now I get to drink your blood daily. But how would you formally start to teach someone?'
Ken said:

The best way to teach is to have the person *do it*. I learned a lot from Disney and from live action. Chuck used to get us live action dance films and we would pick out the extreme positions and outline them. Disney traced a lot from live action. Snow White herself was all rotoscoped. They had the girl act it out, filmed it and traced it off. I don't like to work that way and most animators don't. The best of them put the live action on the moviola and turn it over frame by frame and study it. I did a dance with Gene Kelly – matching him dancing with a little mouse. I did another one of Bugs Bunny matching Jack Carson.

I asked, 'Since dancing is one of your specialties, do you dance it first yourself?'
He said:

I can animate anything I can do – or see somebody do. Mike Maltese used to do these dances – he could do any type of jig step. He would do it slow, kick this toe here and move it out, and down and out, and then add them up – and you could do it. One of the girls in the studio was a dancer – she danced in the *Salome* picture. We could get her, and she would dance, do it, and show me the steps and everything.

But the quickest way is to go to the animation morgue and get a film. We'd get something that Warners had in stock, a guy jumping up into the air – and see how fast

he turns. They're looking at you – then they turn their heads right back again, zoop-zoop-zoop, and they do these spins and all that stuff – and you can see the timing. You don't know how to do it unless you see somebody who does know how to *do it* – do it. Of course you *exaggerate* it a lot in animation.

I learned a lot from Disney model sheets that the guys gave me off and on – about certain takes and speed runs and things. One drawing tells you a whole story. That's the reason Chuck gets pretty good animation. He does the drawing and it's got a lot of action in it. It's got a feeling of what he wants. He's pretty good at that. You could take that one drawing and say, Gee, I can tell what he wants here. He wants this guy to run with his knees up to his chin, just churning away. Sometimes he'll have a guy rearing way back, running like that and you'll know he wants that kind of feeling to it.

I asked him what advice he could give to anybody.

The only advice I know is to think it all out in your mind. Then visualise it the best you can. Then draw it out the best you can. And then test it to *see* if it's right. Unless you have somebody here who can say, 'Oh, throw this drawing out', or 'You need to speed it up here' or 'Put in a couple of in-betweens to slow it down here.'

Ken with Grim Natwick and Art Babbitt
outside our London studio, 1973

Timing is something you just can't tell a person how to do. They've gotta feel that themselves. The only thing I can tell a person to do is just to *animate*.

It's hard for me to sum up much about Ken or his life.

In one way I knew him awfully well, but I only knew the animation part of him. I always talked to him about animation, I had no interest in cars or tennis so I'd get him back to talking about animation. He didn't seem too interested in money, but was always irritated with himself about the California orange groves that he could once have bought for a song and which were now worth millions.

He was a modest, honest man, *very* interested in his work for its own sake. He knew he was good at it, but his drawing limitations always bothered him. He said it was because he started so late. He had to take aim and draw. 'God damn it, Dick, it's *almost* right – but not quite.' He could see it clearly in his head. But he drew funny – everything was funny, and he had a wide range of acting. He had impeccable taste, nothing corny, nothing overdone (no matter how crazy), understated, real judgement.

Producer-Director Bill Hanna (of Hanna-Barbera) was often courting Ken to work on special things for him – 'Ken, you can work on my yacht if you like' – and always told him that it was because he 'had such good taste in his work – perfect taste'.

It's true. Ken could take a gross and stupid gag and when he'd finished animating it, it was no longer gross and stupid, but funny and compelling.

Towards the end Ken said to me, 'Hey, maybe I did have really good taste, after all.'

At the risk of *bad* taste I feel I can include this death scribble I made of Art Babbitt contemplating Ken's husk. I'd never seen a dead person before. Ken wouldn't have minded because he certainly was not there.

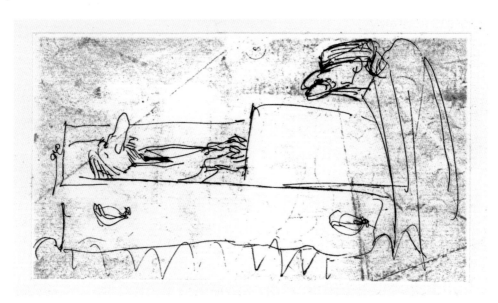

A CHRISTMAS CAROL

I won my first Oscar for a half-hour film of Dickens, *A Christmas Carol*. It was for television, and I got the job because Chuck Jones had liked the *Light Brigade* work very much. He said, 'I want

you to animate *A Christmas Carol* in the style of 1850s illustrations – like *The Light Brigade*.' I said, 'My God, we'll never do it in nine months. We'll never be able to do it in time. Not with all that cross-hatching.' He said, 'No, I've showed them *The Light Brigade* and that's what you gotta do,' and I said, 'Well, can we do it in pencil, just pencil please? Not ink.' And Chuck said, 'Okay.'

Dickens was quite a contrast to the fantasy land of *The Little Island*. The great thing was that we had Ken Harris. He animated an awful lot of Scrooge himself and I caricatured Ken as Scrooge and drew his hands. It was a ridiculous amount of work but we got through it.

Scrooge and the Ghost of Christmas Present

Marley's ghost

107

Note interesting factor whether scenes are very complex or not it averages
out over a period.   CHRISTMAS CAROL POST-MORTEM   972.

ANIMATION AND BACKGROUNDS

FOOTAGE RATE
FULL TIME ANIMATORS

Ken Harris	6 min	31 ft per week	Worked in Pencil. Needed rough inbetweens – Clean – up and final inbetweens
Abe Levitow	3 min 40s	30" " "	Worked in graphite. Needed only one assistant for inbetweens.
Bill Hajee	3 min 16s	16" " "	Worked in chinagraph rough. Needed Purdum and Williams throughout production for clean-up. Final inbetweens.
George Nicholas	1 min 52s	16" " "	Worked in graphite. Needed only minimum clean-up and one assistant for inbetweens.
Hal Ambro	1 min 24s	11" " "	Worked in pencil. Needed rough inbetweens clean-up and final inbetweens.
Sergio Simonetti	1 min 30s	8" " "	Worked in graphite. Needed only one assistant + produced special production work.
Oscar Grillo	33s	8" " "	Worked in graphite. Complex work needed 2 assistants.

PART TIME ANIMATORS   BACKGROUNDS

Dick Williams	2 min 18s	Direction, layout, backgrounds + clean up	Dick Williams	217
Dick Purdum	1 min 24s	Head of clean – up also Storyboard	Janet Chapman	58
Janet Chapman	1 min 36s	FX Animation, backgrounds + crowd anim.	Roy Naisbitt	27
Roy Naisbitt	53s	Layout + overall supervision of Prod.	Dick Purdum	8
			Tony White	10
			Sergio Simonetti	9

Footage charts

When Dick Huemer saw it, he said, 'Marley's ghost made the hair up the back of my neck stand up. So you're still my favourite director.' But he also reacted to the realism, 'What are you doing? Realism?'

And I said, 'Making a living.'

Ward Kimball also reacted, 'Animation is not real, it's an invention, a cartoon.'

Chuck Jones threatened me. He said, 'If you ever go and do a live action film, I'll kill you.' Basically, he was saying – stick with animation.

A Christmas Carol was a big prime-time success and it was considered – because it was so realistic – to be revolutionary.

Receiving my first Oscar from Peter Boyle and Beatrice Arthur

ART BABBITT: HOW TO BREAK THE RULES

Art Babbitt didn't have a Disney philosophy of entertainment or a way to draw – he taught with stick figures.

Now somebody like me, who is a kind of fancy draughtsman, when I had to do stick figures it exposed all my weaknesses, because I couldn't be facile. I had to do just like everybody else – a stick figure.

I remember in one of Art's first classes, I had the worst test out of forty people because I couldn't show off.

Teaching with stick figures is devoid of style so you put in whatever style or preference you have. Art gave you the bones, the structure to be an artist.

Art said, 'I had to make a choice: mechanical, medical, physics, military – or to entertain. I chose to entertain.'

This was a man who meant business.

Art was a contradictory kind of fellow. A very great animator and a wonderful teacher. He was tough as nails but very kind. His patience with his students was beautiful. He was theatrical but at the same time down to earth. An intellectual, well-read person, yet a physically tough marine master sergeant. He was devoted to the craft of animation as developed and practised at Disney's – yet he was the strike leader against Disney in 1941. Self-deprecating, but you knew he knew his worth.

Art's animation dictum: 'First learn the rules and then learn how to break them.'

I've heard that when Art was leading the Disney strike, Walt said to another top man, 'Boy, this guy is a real pain in the ass.' 'Yeah, but he's an awfully good animator,' came the reply. Walt asked, 'But is he really *that* good?' Answer, 'I'm afraid so.'

Art was one of the pioneer animators – one of the discoverers and developers of the 'vocabulary' of animation – but, as a result of his union activities and his battles with Walt, he's been written out of the official histories as someone not really to be mentioned, usually referred to as 'the animator' or 'one of the animators'. However, there has been some recognition in these later years of his contribution to the field.

Like Walt Disney, Art was a country boy from the Midwest. He was born in Omaha, Nebraska, of Russian-Jewish origins, and raised in Sioux City, Iowa. His original name was Babitsky.

Art was the oldest of eight children. He said:

My father was an extremely hard worker – worked long, long hours – and *failed* at every occupation he tried. My mother had eight children, and of the eight, only four survived.

I decided to go to New York because my father had had an accident and became paralysed – and it was up to me to earn some kind of a living for the whole family. I was all of 16 and a half, and *never* for a moment intended to become a cartoonist.

Art's ambition was to be a psychiatrist but in order to provide for his family he took up commercial art, and fell into animation work while doing theatrical commercials. 'This was in 1929, the first sound pictures had just come out and I wanted to be a part of that.' Art got a job at Paul Terry's busy studio.

Paul's idea of making a picture was to take gag A and gag B and gag C – depending upon how successful these gags had been – and put them all together, mixing them up and shaking them in a hat and putting them on a long pan. And that was a picture! The idea was not to make it good – but to make it *fast*. One evening I saw a cartoon with sound that absolutely *floored* me. It was Disney's *Skeleton Dance* and I knew then that that was where I wanted to work.

Disney was rapidly expanding and attracting talent from all over America to work with his already famous characters; Art travelled to the West Coast on a one-way ticket in 1932. He got a job (but only as an assistant animator) by sending a big letter to Walt's secretary to get the boss's attention. 'And by big letter I mean it was approximately twenty by twenty-four feet. I sent it special delivery, registered.' Art said he and Walt never really liked each other from the start. Walt was much more interested in enticing Art's close friend, the brilliant animator Bill Tytla, from New York.

Art did so many in-betweens so fast and so well that after only two days he was promoted to full animator. He was one of the four animators who created the wildly successful short *The Three Little Pigs*. Art and Norm Ferguson and Freddie Moore and Fred Spencer were the young animators who pioneered the development of individual cartoon personalities – like actors – with each animator being assigned a different part in a film.

Art said:

> **Fred Moore was largely responsible for the development of the drawing – the nice juicy, fat appearance of these little pigs – and for giving them character. I did approximately a fourth of *The Three Little Pigs* and that was towards the end of the picture in which I drew the wolf and one of the little pigs (the practical pig). At any rate, that was a breakthrough at this particular time.**

Art's 'psychiatric bent' and analytical mind caused him to buy a 16 mm colour film camera to record and study everyday situations, including studio lunchtime activities – volleyball, walks, etc.

En route to Art's first London seminar

Art's exploration of movement helped him transform Goofy from a minor character into a star. Art said, 'Now Goofy, he was an oaf. He was someone who never knew how stupid he really was. He thought long and carefully before he did anything – and *then* he did it wrong.'

Art wrote an industry-famous 'Character analysis of the Goof' for the other animators. He was the first animator to approach the analysis of a character intellectually: how they felt, moved, what their reactions would be in certain situations.

Art's inventive and charmingly captivating portrayal of a drunken country mouse in *The Country Cousin* won Disney an Oscar. Art said, 'I had noticed that one of the things that is normal for a person who is drunk is that he never stands still in one place – he's always sort of weaving around a little bit. And also that, whether they are or not, his eyes seem to be slightly askew.' Robert D. Feild, author of the 1942 book *The Art of Walt Disney*, called *The Country Cousin* a tour de force. 'For mastery of animation – apart from the technical ingenuity – a point was reached that has never been surpassed.' Feild autographed Art's copy of his book: 'To Art – the greatest animator of them all.'

After Disney picked up the Oscar, Art told me he rebuffed Walt's friendly invitations to his home, saying, 'I don't want to be one of your harem – just a respected employee.' Not a response guaranteed to foster good relations for the future.

Art continued his analytic approach.

I very foolishly thought artists and animators should know how to draw. So I got a model and invited the other guys who worked in my room to come to my house in the evenings for an art class. The young animators were very much interested, and they showed up in droves. I invited eight guys and fourteen showed up. The next week I invited those fourteen and twenty-two guys turned up. I had to seat 'em on the floor and on orange boxes and so on. We had no teacher – so I invited an exceptional art instructor, Don Graham, to give the life drawing classes.

But then Disney heard about this private art class in a home and he called me into his office. He said, 'You know, Art, I understand you've been running this art class in your home.' I said, 'Yes, that's true,' and he said, 'Well, you know, it wouldn't look very good in the papers if it came out that a bunch of Disney cartoonists were drawing naked women in a private home.' So I said, 'Well, what do you suggest?' And he said, 'Well, you can use the sound stage here and set up class in the studio and then it would be all right.'

They started the life classes at the studio and also began filming vaudeville comics, dancers and actors in costume, trying out possible actions that the cartoon characters might perform.

Marjorie Belcher, a 16-year-old dancer, daughter of the owner of a Hollywood dance studio, was filmed as a study for Snow White. Art said, 'I shot Marge with my own 16 mm camera on the studio sound stage.' Many of the quotes in this brief biography are taken from *Animating Art*, a prize-winning television documentary about Art Babbitt made by my wife, Imogen Sutton, in 1987. Writer John Canemaker interviewed Marge in 1994, and showed her this documentary. When Art said on the video, 'The idea of taking live action is not that this action was going to be exactly duplicated in the film, but it sort of gives the animator an idea of how the drapery would behave on Snow White's skirt and things like that,' Marge said, 'Oh yeah? Forgot the movement in the face and the body!'

Art again: 'I didn't know Marge at this time and it was only actually after her live action had been completed for the picture that we met quite accidentally on the street – and a romance developed. For months on end I saw her almost every night, and Marge and I were eventually married.'

Snow White gave Art the opportunity to animate a human character – not Snow White herself, but the Wicked Queen, before she turned into a hag. 'I tried to recall some of the people I've known, some of the women I have observed – or known personally – and tried to take snippets of character that would fit this queen, and use them in my animation.' It was quite a jump from cartoony characters, and nothing like it had been done before, but Art succeeded magnificently.

> We were so interested at the time that in the evenings, after working hours, we would go sneaking around into each other's rooms and look through the drawings to see what the other person was doing. Not that anybody tried to withhold any information – in fact, most of the fellows there were very generous with their discoveries. As soon as they did find out something new, they were always ready to pass it on to the next fellow. So it was a great atmosphere.

Disney worked closely with his top animators and he paid them well. 'In the 30s, the height of the Depression, I was living the life of Riley. I didn't realise how fortunate I was. I was earning a *very* good salary. I had two servants, a large house, *three* cars. What in the world was I going to do with three cars?'

Art said:

> I consider *Pinocchio* the best of the features done by Disney in the so-called golden years of the 30s and early 40s. When I animated Geppetto, I was surprised and pleased because there was an *empathy* – a warmth that I felt – that existed not only between Geppetto and Pinocchio, this wooden character, but I felt a warmth towards Geppetto when I witnessed the film. And I think audiences generally felt that warmth, too.

Walt used the word 'sincere' to praise Art's work on Geppetto and, since then, 'sincere' has been the defining catchword used for the Disney approach to depth of character.

On the next film, *Fantasia*, Art drew on his knowledge of dance. He animated the 'Russian Dance' (with dancing flowers) and the 'Chinese Dance' (with dancing

Art in New York with a temporary neck brace. 'He'd had a run-in with a London bus. I don't know if the bus survived.'

mushrooms) from the *Nutcracker Suite*. The charming mushroom dance, though barely a minute long, is one of the most memorable sequences ever animated. To help himself do it, Art took dance and piano lessons.

When asked if they were on drugs when they made *Fantasia*, Art loved to answer, 'Oh yes, and I personally *was* addicted – to Pepto-Bismol, Feen-A-Mint and aspirin.' *Dumbo* followed, and Art was one of the directing animators, personally animating the Western Union messenger-stork delivering the baby elephant.

By the end of 1940 Marge and Art were divorced. She went on to become half of the famous dance duo Marge and Gower Champion. She and Art remained in touch for the rest of his life. She had left him, but I never heard Art say a critical word about her. The 75-year-old Marge told John Canemaker:

> I think he picked the wrong . . . I mean, what did I know at 17? I wasn't even 18 when I married him. I stayed there about six months and then came to New York with the Three Stooges.
>
> I was in their vaudeville act. I was billed as Snow White. I had a round-trip ticket, but I never went home. Art was on the phone a lot and writing a lot of letters, and then he gave me an ultimatum: either come home and have babies or he was going to divorce me. And he did. I never went to court. I was 19 by then. Anyway, it's all water under the bridge.
>
> Thinking back and analysing it now, having had years of therapy, I think Art was a half-full person. With all his talent and his bright mind, he was a negative person. In some ways his friend Bill Tytla was, too. They both married upbeat ladies. Thank God, or they would have wallowed in despair.

The year after his divorce, Art became involved in the famously bitter animation strike. The animation employees at the studio demanded the right to a closed shop cartoonists' union, and Art was the strike leader. He stated, 'Let's make it clear. I wasn't the only one leading the strike. I happened to be the representative of the cartoonists at Disney's. Our motto was, "Liberté, egalité, closed shoppé".'

After nine weeks, the strike finally ended. And so did the golden age of animation. A union was set up, higher wages were agreed for the lower paid and everyone went back to work. But the dispute had pushed the sides further apart and attitudes had hardened.

A little-known fact is that Art was fired and took Walt Disney right up to the Supreme Court of the United States – and won. Imagine the wear and tear and expense for one man challenging the corporation!

Art told John Canemaker in 1975, 'As far as Disney's politics were concerned, they were medieval! He was a cave-man and an America-firster, as was his brother. I was investigated till hell-wouldn't-have-it by the FBI and the office of Naval Intelligence. My Marine Corps enlistment was cancelled and I had to fight to be taken into the Marine Corps as a buck private.'

When World War II ended, no longer a buck private but now a master sergeant, Babbitt returned home, and went back to Disney's 'to prove a point'. I asked Art if, after four years off at the war, it took him very long to get back into animation mode. He said, 'Oh, about ten minutes.'

At the studio he demanded his same wall-to-wall carpeting and moviola, and the same rate of pay. Disney countered by putting Art to work on a specially recorded dance sequence for a movie that Art didn't know was never intended to be made. Walt and Art passed each other in the halls every day but never again spoke. After a year of this, Art finally decided not to make a career of the conflict and left for France.

Art said:

There was no love between us, but I want to give full credit to the genius of Disney the entrepreneur, a very forceful guy who was a great gambler – ready to risk everything for quality. It took a man like that to pull the whole studio together and to make it work. There was always the search for excellence, even though he didn't quite know what it was; he knew that whatever they were doing could be done better. And he surrounded himself with the best. I would equate him with Louis B. Mayer, which is a hell of an equation. He was the Louis B. Mayer and all we artists who pushed pencils were the Greta Garbos. He was audience-wise. He understood the taste of the American public. Animation would never have reached the peak that it did, if it hadn't been for Walt Disney.

Art was certainly aware that the animation golden age had ended as a result of the dispute. And he knew that it virtually ended the career of his closest friend, Bill Tytla – arguably the greatest Disney animator. Tytla was very friendly with Walt and seems to have reluctantly gone out on strike to support his friend Art. Tytla needed the Disney working structure of excellence in order to thrive and, without it, his animation career and work evaporated. My impression was that Art felt responsible for this.

The 1941 strike left a very deep wound in Art and in the years I knew him he often muttered about Disney. On one occasion, when he was reminiscing, I noticed he was all choked up. Despite their differences Art had a great deal of respect and, I believe, affection for Walt.

In France, Art worked for a while as animation consultant/advisor for Lou Bunin's stop-motion animated puppet film *Alice in Wonderland*. He fell in love and married a Czech artist, Dina Gottliebová. Art told me she had saved her own life and her mother's in the Nazi concentration camps by doing medical drawings of body parts for Dr Mengele's write-ups of his human experiments. Art brought Dina and her mother back to California, where the couple settled and had two daughters.

Art became one of the bright lights of the stylistically revolutionary UPA studio – famous for the *Mr Magoo* cartoons. In the Oscar-nominated *Rooty Toot Toot* (1951) – the story of the 'Frankie and Johnny' song – Art animated the defence attorney, most of Johnny and all of the girl, Frankie. Again, Art's knowledge of dance was displayed; he had the defence attorney and Frankie performing *en pointe* – a terrific piece of modern animation that hasn't dated. The director, John Hubley, told me that Art was the only one of the older animators who was really able to fully understand the new concepts and bring his wealth of knowledge to bear on the new stylistic inventions.

When UPA began to get in to trouble, mostly – or directly – as a result of the McCarthyite Un-American Activities Committee investigations, Art, with his work at UPA and the Disney strike behind him, got branded as a 'commie red'. My knowledge of him was that he was just a 'liberal' fellow – tolerant of dissent.

Art then became a partner at Quartet Films and won over eighty awards for his innovative television commercials. When I met him, he'd spent nine years directing the commercial department of Hanna-Barbera. In 1974 I asked him if he could take a leave of absence to teach us in London. He did, we hit it off, and we worked together for the next fifteen years or so, with Art animating and teaching regularly in-house.

Art was very close to his two daughters but his marriage to Dina was not a happy one. During it he had a nervous breakdown, and he hated to talk about this period of his life. But when I met him he had married Barbara Perry, a star dancer and award-winning actress-comedienne. 'Uncle Arthur', the 'living legend', remained very happily married to Barbara and was a fine stepfather to her daughter, Laurie, for the rest of his life. Never one to carry any fat, he was known at home as 'Bones', and was doted on by Barbara, Laurie, and his two grown-up daughters by Dina, Karin and Michele.

As for his teaching, Art had astonishing lucidity – a surgeon's mind. Most animators are sort of incoherent, non-verbal – unable to tell you what they are doing. But Art had no difficulty in showing how a thing worked. Apart from Preston Blair with his large paperback book on animation, Art was twenty years ahead of other top animators in sharing out knowledge of the fundamentals and secrets of the craft. Before he taught us, he had already given several seminars. He loved to teach and was wonderful at it. He said that teaching and passing on his legacy would be his salvation.

A final patronisation from the Front Room to the Back Room. My totally inexperienced studio manager bids the maestro goodnight.

'The Arthurian Legend' was a formidable professor - who regarded the professional skills of the animator as being equivalent to those of a concert pianist.

Art always said that he could have done better: 'I have no illusions, because every time I look at the work I've done, I cringe, because I see what *could* have been.' Once, when Art was staying with me in London, I yelled upstairs, 'Hey Art, come on down – your *Snow White* stuff is on TV!' Back came, 'Hell no, I don't want to eat my own vomit!'

When he won the prestigious International Animation Film Socicty's Winsor McCay Award in 1974, he grunted, 'An award for longevity.'

He said:

I don't want to be artsy-craftsy. I don't want to be abstract or intellectual. I just want to entertain. Very simply, I want to be, pardon the lack of modesty, a Charlie Chaplin of animation. That's it. If I get that far, it will be a tremendous achievement. I would like to tackle Molière, Boccaccio and Racine – things of that stature.

You have to aim high. Animation has not been touched yet. We're really at the very, very primitive beginnings. It would be wonderful if I could leave a legacy – and I know this is presumptuous – leave technique, mechanics and an inspiration for the future of what to strive for. Then I feel I will have accomplished something – a goal which I can't reach, but one I'm sure somebody in the future can.

Art in action: His first month-long seminar at my London studio was like water in the desert for us.

118

THE PINK PANTHER

My next big break came with Blake Edwards, who was the director and creator of *The Pink Panther*. He said, 'Listen, both Peter Sellers and I are – our careers are in the tank but this is going to be a winner. I want you to really let fly with this thing.' So I grabbed it with both hands.

We had an immediate understanding. I said, 'Can I change this character of the Pink Panther a little, can I stretch him out a bit or make him a little more elegant?'

With the *Panther* title, it was always a gag, it was always with a bomb and it went bang, so I said, 'Can we do it with no gags, can we just do the whole thing with movement?'

Ken Harris was a champion dancer and could animate – really handwrite dances and crazy Hollywood walks. I said, 'We'll go for very fluid movement, do the whole thing just on perform-ance, no gags.'

Blake said, 'Yeah, run with it.'

When we finished, Blake came in and saw it and when he came out of the screening I said, 'Well, what do you think?'

He said, 'Thank you.'

He got as far as the door and I said, 'Is that it?'

Blake said, 'Do you want changes?' and I said, 'No, no.'

He said, 'Right, that's the way I work best and that's the way you work best. We've got a hit.'

And that was it.

Pink Panther rough

GRIM NATWICK: 'GET THE MAIN THING RIGHT'

'Curves are always beautiful to watch . Straight lines give power.'

Grim Natwick – the oldest animator on *Snow White* – made it to 100 years of age. After his centennial dinner celebration in Hollywood, attended by 500 members of the animation community, Grim rang up his much younger colleague Chuck Jones and said, 'I'm not going to go for 200.'

Grim was an excellent draughtsman and designer, but he drew really *rough*. He was also one of the few early animators who had proper art school training. He and I were having dinner in a restaurant in London when I spotted some interesting prints of drawings on the wall. They were terrific, unsentimental but beautiful drawings of children and women by the Austrian artist Egon Schiele. I'd never seen his work nor heard of him before. Grim sidled up from the table and said, 'Oh, that's Egon Schiele – he's my favourite artist. He was around with Klimt in Vienna. Now *he* draws in a f— you way. That's how an animator *should* draw!'

Born Myron Nordveig, Grim was a tall, broad-shouldered, handsome Norwegian from a large family in the lumber region of Wisconsin. He was a star track athlete in high school – a state hurdles champion – and he usually talked about animation in athletic terms.

I was never a great sprinter, but I knew the form of running the hurdles, and form in animation is just as important. I notice that among animators there are either former

athletes or athletics devotees. There's a physical feeling in animation. When I animate a scene, I feel it perfectly. When I make one drawing, I know exactly how that figure feels. I know exactly how it feels to stretch that leg forward – and then I know how those in-betweens are going to feel.

What a publicity photograph! Grim, animator of *Snow White*, with his Snow White looka-like student, Tass Hesom. Grim was a live-in tutor in my studio at the time (1974), and I had a manager type who kept saying, 'Don't publish the picture – *save it! Save it* for later!' Well, here it is – many years later.

Grim with Tass Hesom

After high school Grim studied art in Chicago and then in New York. He became an illustrator of the covers of song sheets until a friend of his lured him to work for a year at William Randolph Hearst's cartoon studio, animating the Hearst newspaper comic strip characters. But Grim wanted to be a painter, not a cartoonist, and he saved his salary and went to Vienna in 1925 to study art there for three years.

When Grim came back to New York in 1928, sound had been added to animated cartoons and the public was wild about them. Grim was enticed into working for Bill Nolan, famous for developing 'rubber hose' animation, which audiences found hilarious. Grim worked with Nolan animating *Krazy Kat*, based on George Herriman's marvellous comic strip. Always confident of his drawing abilities, Grim was a natural freelancer and he next joined Max and Dave Fleischer, animating song cartoons with a high 1920s jazz content – Louis Armstrong, Duke Ellington and Cab Calloway soundtracks.

Grim did the first drawing of Betty Boop for Fleischer Studios and served as an animator on most of the first Betty Boop cartoons. Grim said she started out as a cute little dog and ended up as a woman. She was an instant hit. Grim was a specialist in drawing women and was the pioneer in animating them.

'I guess I was the first person to animate a female character and really try to develop the feminine qualities. The early animation was simply trying to make something funny and if anything popped into your head to make it funny, you did it. We always made 100 drawings before we went to lunch.'

One day at Fleischer's, Grim made 'the first serious animation I ever did'. It was a shot of Betty Boop climbing up a rapidly moving locomotive engine. Grim had her hair being whipped around by the wind and other detailed touches, which caught the eye of the young Walt Disney. Walt's brother, Roy, took Grim out to dinner for a week but Grim went to work for Disney's former partner, Ub Iwerks, who'd just set up his own shop. Grim went with Ub because 'the rumour in the east was that Iwerks was the real genius of the Disney studio'.

I did this scribble in the mid-70s of Grim in his mid-80s.

Iwerks was the designer of Mickey Mouse, the sole animator of the first Mickey Mouse shorts and the designer and animator of the first *Silly Symphonies,* including *The Skeleton Dance.* Grim said, 'Iwerks could do everything well. He could draw like a fiend. He'd make a few drawings, then run down to the basement to work on his multiplane camera – well before Disney's had one.' This left Grim upstairs virtually running the place.

Incidentally, my old school friend Carl Bell, a Disney devotee who spent most of his professional life in animation at the Disney studio, recently sent me this:

Forty years ago we were building the 'Art of Animation' exhibits at Stage 4 at Disney's. I was looking at an 8 mm loop of *Steamboat Willie* and standing beside me was the technical director of the exhibits, white-haired Ub Iwerks. Having read a bit of pertinent information in a French volume, *Le Dessin animé,* I remarked, 'I understand you were partially responsible for the creation of Mickey Mouse.' 'Partially?' he retorted. '*Entirely*!'

But Ub didn't have Disney's genius for story or his dramatic sense or business skills and his 'Flip the Frog' series (Grim was the main animator) wasn't popular. Later Iwerks reconciled with Walt, but naturally things were never the same between them.

After three years with Ub on unsuccessful stuff, Grim approached Walt. 'Someone told me that if you'd ever turned Walt down, he'd never hire you.' Story man Ted Sears talked to Walt and Grim was hired. Apparently Walt made a note in his diary that Grim had been hired – a most unusual action for him, which supports the view he had long had his eye on Grim to tackle female lead characters. This was in 1934 and Grim's first job at Disney was animating a long, sustained scene of a girl about to be chosen as festival queen, a sort of rehearsal for Snow White. This was for the Silly Symphony *The Cookie Carnival*.

Grim told me he animated a scene of Mickey Mouse with an eagle in *Alpine Climbers* which was used as a model for new animators trying out at the studio. They had to try to match Grim's skill and inventiveness. He was very proud of this.

After several Mickeys and *Silly Symphonies*, Grim came in on the early development of the princess Snow White. Grim said:

They didn't want her to look like a princess. They wanted her to look like a little girl who could *be* a princess. So instead of a little crown, she had a little bow in her hair – and with the hair we did many things. I had a lot to do with the designing of it because I would try things myself. They allowed me two months of experimental animation before they ever asked me to animate one scene in the picture.

There's this old saying: 'Success has many fathers – but failure is an orphan.' Veteran animator-director-story-chief Dick Huemer rang me up one day when he was 80 and asked, 'Is it true that Grim goes around saying that he animated Snow White?' 'Yes.' 'Oh dear . . . because I was in the same room as Ham Luske and I watched Ham do it.'

Research shows that Hamilton Luske was the official overall supervisor-director-designer in charge of the princess and that he directed the live action reference filming of the girl, and animated some establishing scenes himself. Grim seems to have done the majority of the work, however, along with some other artists. Shamus (James H.) Culhane, who worked on marching dwarfs at the time, told me that you can always spot Grim's scenes because the hands are so well drawn. 'Grim was the only one who drew well enough to really handle the hands well.'

Michael Barrier, in his book *Hollywood Cartoons*, reports that the animation analysis instructor Don Graham said to one of his Disney studio classes, 'How can anyone say what can be done with a human figure until someone tries? Grim is the only one that has seriously tried it around here, and he hasn't had a chance to show it in a picture yet. But he has the knowledge.'

What is clear, I think, is that Grim had a more worldly and artistically sophisticated approach to Snow White, as opposed to the more cartoony, larger-headed approach of Luske.

I remember Grim starting work by swirling his pencil around on the paper for ten minutes – kind of like a baseball pitcher warming up.

Pencil drawing of Betty Boop
by Grim Natwick (1974)

There is a particular shot in *Snow White* that has always inspired me – as a way, a clue to handling realistic characters – and it turned out that Grim did it. Grim said, 'The best animation generally that I ever did was where she runs down the stairs. It was too risky to rotoscope, so I had to animate that, and it turned out to be one of the nicest . . . and that's what Williams thought and that's why he wanted me to come to London.'

Grim said:

We were too young to know what the hell we were doing. I don't know how we did it. I don't think anyone else does, really. I never had any gripe with Disney's. It was a great place to work, terrific experience, and, I believe, the greatest college of animation in the world. Disney had only one rule: whatever we did had to be better than anyone else could do it, even if you had to animate it nine times – as I once did.

I don't know why, but I gather from some things Grim told me, and from hearsay, that he had some trouble with Freddie Moore about how to draw Mickey Mouse in the 'Sorcerer's Apprentice' section of *Fantasia*. In 1939 Grim went back to Max Fleischer to direct and animate on *Gulliver's Travels* in Florida. Then in 1941 he went back to the West Coast and joined Walter Lantz to animate girls on Lantz's *Swing Symphonies* and then worked on Woody Woodpecker cartoons. In the 50s (and in Grim's 60s) he went with the modern breakaway UPA studio, working on Mr Magoo and groundbreaking shorts – then to UPA's New York studio to do TV work and commercials. When UPA's animation studio folded, Grim freelanced for a while, then went back to California to paint. And that's where I captured him to be tutor-in-residence at my London studio. He also started animating again and became a celebrated guest at international animation festivals and wrote articles. He won the Winsor McCay Award for animation in 1975.

Grim was married and divorced once and had a daughter who must have been well into her 60s when I knew her father. But however fond he was of women, he spent most of his long life as a bachelor.

Animator and animation chronicler John Canemaker put it nicely about Grim: 'A vigorous man, with a mind that cracks like a brand-new whip.' Grim was a marvellous raconteur and wordsmith – a very stimulating character. The only problem I found with learning from him was that like a lot of the men who grew up inside the medium that they were developing, he tended to generalise and be philosophic about it all – instead of being specific about 'what do I do first, then what do I do to get a certain result?' He always used sports analogies – 'It's like a baseball pitcher struggling to develop his knuckle ball . . . finally it all comes out right and you wonder what all the fuss was about in the first place.'

But the most valuable advice from Grim that I always remember is, 'Get your *main* thing right, *real* right – and it doesn't matter too much about the other bits.'

Grim said:

> There's a vocabulary of 2,000 things – just as if there were 2,000 words – that you have to learn about animation. If you've got that vocabulary, you're a great animator. If you have 200 of them you could get by today. A lot of animators are getting by with a very small vocabulary. What do you know about animation today and what will you know ten years from now? You'll find that in ten years you'll be able to do in one hour what you take a day to do now. That's because you keep piling knowledge upon knowledge till pretty soon you have 500 words in that vocabulary that will make it a lot easier.

With Grim – 'Man watching another man working'

10-24-76

Dear Dick:
    Unbelievable as it is I yesterday discovered something about animation that I have been doing for a long, long time and yet was not, until yesterday, ~~conscious of~~ aware of—

In my animation and especially in humourous animation I am always unconsciously animating shapes, squares, triangles, oblongs, circles. In my first roughs I hurle the shapes onto the drawing paper, then contrast them in turn with shapes that (by flipping) produce comic movement. Unconsciously I probably include all the letters of the Greek alphabet:

"A" against "T" or L against "O"

I had several rough drawings spread out on my table and suddenly I said, 'Hell! These are only a lot of traditional shapes.'

The figures are fitted into them

Basically I am using forms that are well known to every child. The added detail that turns the shape into a character does not alter the basic pattern. It is an interesting fact - an important one, I believe. I think dull animation is dull because it lacks an underpinning of something that gives the mind a psychological jolt.

I am very serious about this. I know you are interested in animation theory so I thought I would pass it along—

128

10-24-76

Dear Dick,

Unbelievable as it is I yesterday discovered something about animation that I have been doing for a long, long time and yet was not, until yesterday, aware of –

In my animation, and especially in humorous animation, I am always unconsciously animating shapes, squares, triangles, oblongs, circles. In my first roughs I hurl the shapes onto the drawing paper, then contrast them in turn with shapes that (by flipping) produce comic movement. Unconsciously, I probably include all the letters of the Greek alphabet:

'A' against 'T' or 'L' against 'O'

I had several rough drawings spread out on my table and suddenly I said, 'Hell! These are only a lot of traditional shapes.'

= (Drawing of a square, triangle, oblong, semicircle)

The figures are fitted into them – (Drawing of a person drawn in a triangle – person drawn in an oblong)

Basically I am using forms that are well known to every child. The added detail that turns the shape into a character does not alter the basic pattern. It is an interesting fact – an important one, I believe. I think dull animation is dull because it lacks an underpinning of something that gives the mind a psychological jolt.

I am very serious about this. I know you are interested in animation theory so I thought I would pass it along –

Grim thought most animation factories 'are just trying to make a quick buck so that they can make another quick buck – and it's a shame'.

He said: 'I have ideas on what can be done. I don't think animation has even been tried yet.'

Good luck. Great luck. Now I'll lock up my 'studio' for the night –
Best – GRIM –

Grim lived from 1890 to 1990.

Self-portrait of a man who is always working

EMERY HAWKINS:

'GO FROM A TO X TO B – NOT A TO B'

EMERY

'I can't resist the temptation to take the formula and change it.'

Ken Harris said to me one day, 'Hey, Dick, you know who probably the best animator is?' 'Who?' 'Emery Hawkins – you ought to work with him! He was with us at Warners for a while and he was terrific. And he never stopped thinking about it all – always inventing new actions for Bugs Bunny, etc.'

Who in the world knows about Emery Hawkins? Well, Milt Kahl said this about his work: 'Very imaginative and ingenious.'

Art Babbitt: 'Masterful, I've never seen anything to top it in any animated cartoon any-where at any time! It's original: It's a tour de force! I sent Emery a fan letter – the first one I've ever sent in my life to anyone.'

Grim Natwick: 'Emery Hawkins is the only animator I know who can go completely insane in his animation and make it seem rational!'

They're talking about Emery's animation of a metamorphosing monster in a taffy pit in the *Raggedy Ann & Andy* feature film which I was supposed to have directed, but didn't. I did to start with, and Emery was able to complete three-quarters of his masterpiece before we were both removed from the fray by panic-stricken business people inexperienced in the field. For me, it was early days and I could write it off to experience, but in Emery's case it was tragic.

He was at the summit of his career and about to achieve the fulfilment and recognition that had, for reasons which will become clear, eluded him – and he'd almost broken his health working on this sustained piece of comic invention, nothing like it ever seen before or since. It was like a spun-out shaggy-dog story, and when it approached the climactic payoff he was removed from the job so a couple of young beginner animators could bat the rest out fast and cheap. And they did. So: no punchline, no climax, no conclusion to a wonderful, hilariously inventive build-up. I don't want to talk about the picture here but I have to, somewhat, in order to talk about Emery and his originality and brilliance. After the picture came out, the chief executive flew to London and said, 'Well, Dick, you were right and now we'd like to do it again, *your* way.'

Emery was not famous in the industry for the very reason he was great. Change. He was the master of change. In his life he restlessly kept changing.

Emery: 'I've always been a renegade, to be honest. I've moved about forty-seven times at different jobs. I shuttled between studios. I worked a number of times at all of them. I'd do little parts and bits of a picture and then off I'd go. I was bobbing. Couldn't stay put. My father was like that.'

Emery was part Native American and I always thought that his nomadic ancestry might have something to do with his moving around and his supple imagination.

These sketches give some idea of Emery's unique mastery of 'change'. The monster is the taffy pit.

Emery was born Emery Otis Hawkins in a little town called Jerome, on the side of an Arizona mountain riddled with mine shafts. Emery's father, C. T. Hawkins, was a cattleman who is in the record books, voted 'The All-round Cowboy of Arizona' for two years running. Emery said his dad 'won everything – roping, riding, throwing. He could play a fiddle and jig and call a dance all at once!'

Emery's parents divorced. His mother married a cabinet-maker and they moved to Hollywood with Emery. Emery was always drawing. 'I always did animation. I did it on notebooks, figured it out on flip books.'

When he was 16, Emery went to the Disney studio with a scene he had animated of a clown walking. Emery said, 'They didn't think I had done it.' They turned him away saying, 'We don't want copy work.'

Emery's next stop was the Charles Mintz studio where they *did* believe him and he became an animator. He went back to Disney's in 1932 and this time he was hired.

Disney apparently recognised Emery's unique originality because Emery told me he worked just with Walt himself. Walt used Emery as a kind of extension on things he wanted to explore. Then he got Emery to make changes for him on other animators' work. Emery told animation chronicler John Canemaker in 1976:

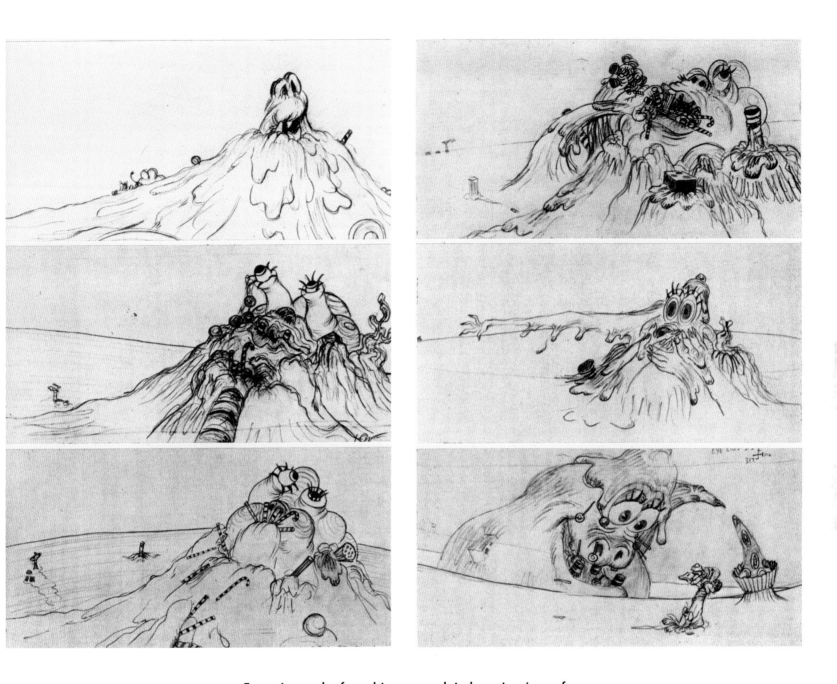

Emery's roughs from his uncompleted masterpiece of
a 'taffy pit' monster of greed devouring itself

I found it oppressive. I would spend weeks trying to do something and still get it to look like the other bloke had done it. It was just not fun. I guess I'm too stupid to work with formulas. I just can't resist the temptation to take the formula and change it. Everything I've ever done, I've always changed changes. Change, change, change! Try to push a thing, stretch it, go further. Lots of times this didn't go over because they had fixed characters with fixed walks with so many beats. And I was always fighting that.

In John Canemaker's book *The Animated Raggedy Ann & Andy* (1977), Warner director Friz Freleng remembers working with Emery at MGM on a Katzenjammer Kids film in the late 1930s.

Emery had to animate a short six-foot scene of a chick carrying a large tomato. Well, by the time he got through, it was up to thirty feet of the most gorgeous animation. He had that little bird going up hills and losing his balance and trying to hold on to the tomato – everything – and no repeats. It was so beautiful I cut some other scenes out to keep it in the picture.

Emery moved studios so many times it's hard to keep track, but he said he left Disney during the 1941 strike and went over to Walter Lantz – then back to Disney in 1944 – then over to Warner Bros. – then MGM – then to the little independent studios.

In the 1950s he'd bus in to New York from his home in Los Angeles to deliver and pick up work from his friends John Hubley and Jack Zander at their commercial studios. Emery's commercials animation was full of 'change' and invention – the most interesting animated commercials I've ever seen.

When *Raggedy Ann & Andy* started up in New York, Emery arrived in his usual cowboy hat, string tie and leather boots to make his deal with production manager Shamus Culhane. 'God damn you, Culhane! That Nicolaides book [*The Natural Way to Draw*] you gave me has screwed me up for twenty-five years!'

Emery told John Canemaker in 1976:

I never got past the second lesson (The Comprehension of Gesture) because I got hung up on gesture. I'd sit near a bus stop in my car, draw people waiting for buses and fill up the back of my car with roughs – studying the core and the contour and the mass and the gesture of a figure until I could see it in my sleep. And when I got through I couldn't animate the same as I used to.

I ended up having to go to 'extremes'. For instance, I'd make the end drawing or the middle drawing and build from there. But it destroyed that thing where you make a loose little soft drawing and the next and the next so you end up with the action. I felt I had to get the guts out of it and get *this* thing first!

For years, animating, I had made a soft, light line and then gone over it and made it clean. I got pretty good results but it was a terrible strain on my nerves. After the Nicolaides book, I stopped animating that way and started drawing those *rough* figures of people – how the figure is shaped and how it bends getting into poses, how the neck and torso work. It started getting fascinating and I could see it in Daumier's work and other artists. It's an *alive* thing!

Now I animate *every* way: backwards, forwards – and then straight ahead. Upside down, in and out, this way, *every* way. Every scene needs a different kind of thing. I envy animators who animate only one way because it kind of settles the nerves and makes problems easier.'

Emery's self-caricature as his candy-pit greed monster

Emery was fascinating to talk to. He had such a different take on things. He never said what you would expect. When I was rattling on at him in a café in New York, he said, 'The trouble is, Dick, you're speaking *you* and I'm hearing *me*.' 'Huh?' 'You're visualising you – and I'm hearing me while you're saying it.'

We talked about drawing not being a language of the tongue, and he said, 'If you haven't developed the language to express yourself – all the education in the world won't help you.'

Here's the main thing I got from Emery. 'Don't go from A to B – go somewhere *else* on the way from A to B. Go from A to X to B. Go from A to K to B.'

The thing that has always intrigued me is the actual *process* of the forms changing. I was always fascinated with the idea of not going directly from one thing to another but going by way of something else. So that you wouldn't know what you were seeing.

135

Things move in *parts*. Work on interesting moves in *parts*. Parts move interestingly – one part against another. Move just one part at a time.

As well as his happy marriage, Emery had a good relationship with his two sons and his grandchildren. In his final years, he suffered from a combination of Parkinson's and Alzheimer's diseases. But I saw him near the end and he was still right there, peeking out through it all.

Emery was a pure artist. He said, 'It's not a business – it's an *expression*.'

'The only limit in animation is the person doing it. Otherwise, there is no limit to what you can do. And why *shouldn't* you do it?'

CHRISTMAS CARDS

Over the years Christmas cards
were an illustration of the
people working at the studio
and its work.

WHO FRAMED ROGER RABBIT

My next huge opportunity came in 1986 with *Who Framed Roger Rabbit*.

Disney had developed the project for seven years and Robert Zemeckis worked on it when he was younger. Then he said, 'I'll see you guys later,' and left.

At that time Bugs Bunny was the top animation character in the world so why, for a start, would they try and do a grey rabbit?

So the thing languished. Then Zemeckis did *Back to the Future*, which was very big. He was a protégé of Steven Spielberg and wanted to get the rights from Disney, so they – Spielberg and Disney – had made a temporary marriage and were looking for an animation director. But I didn't want to do it.

With my painting of Roger Rabbit at AMPAS in LA in 2013

I said to Zemeckis, 'I love the early Disney movies – *Snow White*, *Dumbo*, *Bambi*, *Pinocchio*, *Fantasia*. But I thought the animation in *Mary Poppins* was awful. The cartoons look pasted on. They look like they're on a piece of glass in front of the characters.' I said to Zemeckis, 'You're mixing the two realms and they don't fit. It demeans the animation and it also wrecks the live action. This pasted-on business is just no good.'

He replied, 'But have you seen *Star Wars – Return of the Jedi*, with the motorbikes flying through the forest?'

He said, 'Industrial Light & Magic have figured out a way of printing the cartoon thing, the drawn thing, so that it fits into the live action. They expose it differently, so you've got the different levels working.' And I said, 'Well, then we can do it.' And then Zemeckis said, 'In *Mary Poppins*, the penguins are actually animated beautifully because they got the eyelines right.'

So when Bob Hoskins is looking at the animated characters in *Who Framed Roger Rabbit*, you believe he is interacting with them. He had this wonderful ability to stop his eyes right at the belt line which was at the level with the Rabbit's eyeline. I asked him, 'How did you get that concentration?' He said, 'Don't make me think about it or I won't be able to do it.'

Zemeckis said that the animation directors always insisted on having a locked-off camera, so the camera was still, which meant that the animators didn't have to turn the characters much. He told me, 'I'm trying to shoot a modern movie where the camera's moving all the time,' and I said, 'That's no problem.' He said, 'But all the animation directors we've talked to say you have to have it locked off.' And I said, 'Because they're lazy bastards.'

He asked, 'But isn't it more work?' And I said, 'What do you think animation is? It's nothing but work. That's our job, turning things in space.'

It was a very expensive technique, this kind of moving camera technique, because it meant that we had to print every frame of the film that we were going to animate. They would print it at Industrial Light & Magic in San Francisco, mail it over to us and we'd have these big drawings, big pictures for each frame – you'd just put a piece of paper on it, and draw a rabbit in there.

Animation is time-consuming, but that was *really* time-consuming – that's why there were so many people on it. After every hand-drawn film, they store all the drawings, and with *Roger Rabbit* they had about three times as many as normal.

It wasn't 3D, more like 2-and-a-half D. The animation worked because the characters weren't quite round. We back-lit, with a sort of rim light, and I'd have to draw them on. It was quite a simple thing, as I figured out. Because a lot of the live action was blurred, the images were blurred naturally. At twenty-four frames a second, it was just going to be a blur. So they said, 'You can't put a hard-edged piece of animation into that', and I said, 'Well I already have – strangely enough, on a commercial I animated for Disney, with all the Disney characters playing football' – and I'd broken all the rules.

I said, 'I can prove it, let's give it a try.' So we did a test sequence – a sort of obstacle course the Rabbit would have to deal with – in the live action world. We filmed an actor in a back alley with beer cans and neon lights flashing and I drew the Rabbit coming down the stairs and he lit up as a car went past, then bashed into a bunch of garbage cans at the bottom. All we did was just put a string on the garbage cans, pulled them away, and it looked as though the Rabbit had knocked them over. And then a marvellous guy called Ken Ralston at Industrial Light & Magic did all the effects and it worked. The two realms came together.

Michael Eisner, who headed Disney then, was very dubious about the thing. So he took the test – it was about a minute and a half – home to his private screening room and invited the neighbourhood kids in and ran it and said, 'Do you think I should invest in this?' And all the kids said, 'Yeah, yeah, yeah!' And that's how they made *Roger Rabbit*.

My favourite part of the film is the opening. Bob Zemeckis used to come in and say, 'You're not still working on that opening are you?' And I'd say, 'Well.' And he'd say, 'Well, just do a good solid Tom and Jerry, just do it like that. Don't make a big deal of it.' Of course, I realised that this was the part of the film that was being left to me, so I started working at night on it, and Bob came in at one point and said, 'Oh God, Dick, you're not still working on that opening? You know, if they catch you doing it, they'll fire you.' Translation – I'll fire you. But I'd done so much of it that it went through and I was very pleased. I knew it was going to work. I did the transition to the live action with the Rabbit in the fridge and the baby throwing his fit and he gooses the girl and so on. Although I was directing the animation of the entire film, that was the end of my own animation – it was my favourite bit because there wasn't any live action.

But I also worked all over the picture. For instance, when Bob Hoskins is driving his car, he was sitting on a sort of makeshift kind of car, without sides or anything, and we drew a car on top of it, every frame. Or when the Rabbit's drinking whisky – George Gibbs made a thing like a little lever and the lever 'drank' whisky, a glass of whisky. So you'd have this crazy-looking thing and the actor would be there and I'd draw a rabbit over the top of the lever. And then, as for the Rabbit, we'd do it in pencil and then they'd Xerox that on to celluloid, then they'd paint the thing and then

GREAT GREAT GUYS TERRIFIC! KILL THE WORLD!

Caricature of Bob Zemeckis

we'd give extra little mattes to make it look round. It was very simple. Afterwards, they went around saying how difficult it was. But it was just back-breaking work.

I ended up with a Special Achievement Oscar and sharing the Special Effects one with George Gibbs and Ken Ralston. So I got two Oscars for that one and by then we were really rolling.

MILT KAHL:

'EVERYTHING DRIVES THE PERFORMANCE'

'I knew enough about it that I could do practically anything'

Milt said, 'If I thought there was anything nice to be said about me, other people ought to say it.'

Well, I'm going to do it right here, and so are some others.

'He was a Zeus among animators,' said Grim Natwick.

At Disney's he was known as 'King Kahl' or simply, 'God'. Like God, he had many aspects. He was everywhere at once with his works.

Milt influenced the style and designed and animated the establishing performances of many of the main characters in the Disney classics from *Pinocchio* on through *Bambi*, *Song of the South*, *Cinderella*, *Alice in Wonderland*, *Peter Pan*, *Lady and the Tramp*, *Sleeping Beauty*, *One Hundred and One Dalmatians*, *The Jungle Book*, *The Sword in the Stone*, *The Aristocats*, *Robin Hood* and *The Rescuers*.

The great animator Marc Davis – like Milt, one of Disney's 'Nine Old Men', and famous for his animation of Cruella de Vil in *One Hundred and One Dalmatians* – said, 'You know about Milt, you kind of had to give him a start on a character – we did a lot of work first, before he got to it . . . but once you did give it to him and well, once he got it . . . he *is* the world's greatest animator!'

Milt generally avoided self-promotion, only muttering, 'Well, I'm not like a lot of those lazy bastards, I really do think I work harder.'

I never got to work with Milt. Several times he wanted me to go to Disney's but for various reasons I never did. The closest we ever got to working together was after he left Disney's. His response to my asking if he'd work with me was always 'I'm not saying no.' But I never quite had the situation ready for it. And by the time I started my three years as a Disney/Spielberg director on *Roger Rabbit*, he was near the end of his life.

I scribbled this of Milt when he was lecturing us at my London studio. Milt is saying, 'Don't listen to Dick, he's too technical.'

Shortly before Milt died in 1987, I recorded a long interview with him, and during it I asked him about his influence on the Disney style. He said:

A friend told me in a letter one time that it seemed remarkable to her how a person as vividly individual as I am could adapt himself to the Disney style so readily. It struck me as kind of funny because I don't think there is a Disney style. There isn't a style that exists that I know of, and if there is one, there was nothing for me to adapt to because I had as much to do with developing it as anybody did over the years. I felt a little bit like the chess champion of the world at one time who was a Franco-Russian by the name of Alexander Alekhine. Someone, an onlooker, in the middle of a game said to him – 'Mr Alekhine, that isn't a book move you made there.' Alekhine said, 'I *am* the book.'

Milt didn't want to be anybody's teacher, but he would tell you stuff. If he heard a well-formulated question, he'd give you a wonderful answer. He regarded most animators – you could almost say all animators – almost – as lazy bastards. He wasn't a lazy bastard, and he knew he wasn't. He would often say, 'I really do feel I'm not a lazy bastard – like these lazy bastards I'm working with. Of course, now, Frank Thomas – Frank was way better – *way, way* above these run-of-the-mill guys! A different story! I'd check with him a lot – throw drawings back and forth a lot. We've always worked pretty closely over the years.'

Fortunately, Milt didn't regard me as a lazy bastard. He knew I was sincere and had some stuff going for me. He was more than flattering about my drawing – and always encouraged me to go my own direction. I'd say to him, 'You're the best ever. Help me! Please tell me how you do this or how do you do that?' and he would tell me. Or he'd stutter for a while. People would make fun of him stuttering. That was stupid because when Milt was stuttering he was trying to formulate, prepare the answer. So you were a damn fool if you didn't hang on. And out would come the answer. But he didn't like to think of it that way. He didn't like to think of it technically.

But you still had to push him about the technical side of things. He'd say, 'Well, you know . . . you know. Yeah, of course everyone knows that – well, you just do it, you know. You gotta do that, you know.' I'd say, 'No, really, Milt, I don't know.' Then he'd duck it by saying, 'Look, you just give the performance, that's the thing. That's what's important!' 'Yes, yes, but I want to know *how* you do such and such.' But he would also say, 'If you ask questions, you find out what you want to know. If you're lucky enough to ask someone who knows.' I'd say, 'Yes, so I'm asking.' And then out would come eloquent pearls of 'how to' information – always ending with, 'Yeah, but all that's important is the performance – the essence of the character, the play. Everything else is just a means to an end. Like the drawing. Your drawing is just a means to an end.'

Milt said, 'I'm not one of those people who draws compulsively. I don't draw unless I have to. I don't really enjoy it. I don't mind it, but I got my kicks at the studio by putting a performance on the screen.'

Milton Kahl was born in San Francisco in 1909. His father was German. Kahl means 'bald' and is a local name from the Cologne area. His mother was of English extraction. I always thought Milt was a combination of Germanic concentration and precision and English humour.

Milt said:

My father had a little talent but he wasn't the least bit an educated man and didn't have any artistic training at all. But he used to do the newspaper ads for the limousine rental company that he worked for. I don't remember how good they were because I was awfully young – 8, 9, 10 years old at the time. My parents were terribly poor. If they could have a little bit more money coming in, they had no objections to it.

I used to draw on toilet paper quite a bit. Motorcycles. And I remember I saw a thing my grandparents had saved when I was 7. I had done a Mexican with a sombrero and

then I finished it up by putting a part of a lace curtain over it. I thought that was kind of good. But there was really nothing to indicate what I would become.

My mother was a dear. But later I had a stepfather who was like a little bantam rooster – vulgar rooster. We didn't get along very well. I left home as soon as I could.

I didn't even finish high school. I went to work for a photo engraving outfit and then I got a job on the *Oakland Post-Inquirer* in the art department – doing paste-ups and layouts. I'd fancy up the corners, retouch them. Then, that got me to drawing once in a while for the theatrical page or sports page. Then I worked for the *San Francisco Bulletin*. The stock market crashed and the *Bulletin* was sold and they didn't keep anybody. I ended up working for Fox West Coast Theatres doing advertising pictures and cards for the front of streetcars.

I was always a little scared of Milt. Because he was for real. He was the authority. That's always scary. As if you were talking about the violin to Isaac Stern. You'd be careful. He would call me a kiss-ass now and then when I'd get the questions wrong. But you could yell back at him. Mostly, he took me very seriously. He thrilled me.

Milt didn't want to mess around. He hated being intellectual about his work. But of course he was. He could tell you the gravity pressure on a leaf. He didn't want to be quoted. He didn't want to mess around with what he was serious about. So you had to have the right key for the lock. It had to be a well-formulated question and he would give a well-formulated answer.

I (and others) could always spot his scenes in the pictures – which Milt could never quite believe. He'd say, 'How can you tell? Once it's gone through the mill it gets all flattened out. It's nothing different.' One time I told him, 'Look, it's very obvious – it's in the proportions of the drawings and in the proportion of the movements.' He stopped dead. 'You're getting smarter.'

One of the last times I saw Milt, I told him, 'You know, I was raised on the great American illustrators of the 30s and 40s who worked for the *Saturday Evening Post* and *Collier's* magazines. There were about ten famous ones, and your work somehow reminds me of one of them who did a lot of animals and riders. Did you ever see the work of Fred Ludekens?' 'Fred Ludekens! My God, he was my teacher and friend! We had a studio together!'

There was an aesthetic similarity of style. There was an analytical thing in the drawing; precision, clarity and shape. 'See, Milt, I'm not so stupid. Now will you believe me when I say I can always spot your work?'

Milt was always encouraging me to do my own personal, more unconventional work, which he liked – but I wanted the knowledge first.

About his slight hump back, Milt said:

My 'posture' is partly occupational and partly genetic. I don't know. Anyway, all I know is that it is there. I went and had a physical one time and the doctor told me I'd had rickets when I was a child – and my mother hit the ceiling when I told her about it. Oh, she got so mad.

'But Milt all we want is to learn how to slow in & out' –
'Buzz off and do your own thing, Williams'

By 1934 I was a commercial artist and I wanted to get into magazine illustration, but that field died. Why go to Disney's? Sounded like leprosy, but my business started falling off. The Depression caught up with me and I got a letter from the Disney studio with an opportunity to try out. Ham Luske was one of the key Disney animators at that time and he'd worked with me on the *Oakland Post-Inquirer*. Ham had drawn illustrations for the sports section. He suggested me as a possibility – so I gave it a try.

I was 25 years old in 1934 when I joined Disney at the Hyperion studio. Actually, I was awfully excited about working at the Disney studio. I had seen the *Three Little Pigs* picture and that really captivated me. That thing swept the country. I was quite captivated by the purity of the colours too. When you get colour that is projected and has a transparency to it – it has a lot more vibrance than colour on a painting.

I had never considered going into this medium myself, but I seemed to be ideally suited for it. I was fascinated by the medium. But when I got down there, they had me doing in-betweens. I was just making in-between lines and not really drawing. But I realised that was temporary. I know it sounds a little egotistical, but I turned out to be made for that medium. I used to do a lot of still lifes and portraits and that sort of thing. I had done a lot of art school – but I think I really started to draw – really *draw* – when I came to the studio.

The studio was awfully small. There were only, I think, 125 people employed there, including janitors. So it was a small place, a very small operation.

I asked Milt, 'What was the most valuable thing about your experience at Disney? Obviously, there were some hard times and things that tried on you a lot but you stayed there all those years – forty-two years.' He shot back:

Walt. He is the answer. Disney contributed a terrific amount. You have a very strange combination there. You have a guy who, in the first place, is a genius, and in the second place he owns the place, and he owns it the hard way. My God, he went through hell year after year to keep this place going; to keep this dream of his alive. How the hell do you come up with somebody like this? It's a strange phenomenon that only happens once in a great while.

Walt was an absolutely wonderful storyteller. And he had the ability to get things out of people that they weren't capable of. He really *did*! That sounds funny but he could really do it. As for the director, Walt was really the director. You'd look at the storyboard

and, God, you had paper all over the floor when he got through. He controlled everything. Believe me, he was a hard man to please. But I had a hard time pleasing myself. If I liked it, well, that was good enough for me.

Walt was always being told he was spending too much money. He had a favourite four-letter word for that, and he'd say, 'Awww, *shit!*' He was always going over budgets. He'd be infuriated with his brother, Roy, who would be trying to keep things on a sensible basis financially. Walt just wouldn't be shackled with anything like that. It seemed like everything he touched turned to gold, like King Midas. It's amazing really, because he didn't think about it. I don't think Walt ever in his life entered into any project because primarily it was going to make money.

Walt was quite a phenomenon – the fact that a guy like that existed. It was amazing to me over these years that he kept all these very diversified artists together – people who were rugged individualists, people to whom a group effort was foreign – and he brought them all together and got good results and made good pictures.

I just did what Walt told me to, I figured you had to make the damn thing good. It was his ass, you know, to use the vernacular. We gave everything we had, and we could, but still there is a lot of difference in having all the financial responsibility, and not having it.

There's a tendency nowadays to find something that works and use it forever. That's a rotten way of looking at the business. When a bad picture is a financial success you can't argue about it. You don't have enough basis for arguments – not with the businessmen. With Walt, you would have. He wouldn't be thinking about it in dollars and cents. Walt didn't like to chew his cabbage twice. In my wildest dreams I can't imagine Walt saying, 'Well, you know, there's nothing wrong. These things make a lot of money, you know.' He could be so goddamned contemptuous of something that he didn't like, or something that he didn't think was good, and they'd just work their tails off to get something good for him.

There was never any lack of respect on my part – and he always respected me, too. He always knew that I meant what I said. He wasn't a good guy for a yes-man or a toady to cope with – because if you said, 'Oh yes, Mr Disney,' or 'Oh yes, Walt, that's a swell idea,' he'd think about it – and the next day, he'd figured out it was a lousy idea.

We had a lot of *talent* there. I think you learn from everyone. A place like Disney – especially in the old days when you had Freddie Moore and Norm Ferguson and Ward Kimball and Ham Luske and all these awfully talented guys – you couldn't help but have these guys rub off on you.

I'd been at the studio about a year and a half, two years, when *Snow White* went into animation. Jimmy Algar, Louie Schmitt, Eric Larson and I had a unit that did all of the little animals. The animals were just decoration, so it wasn't any big thing. I got a lot out of Eric. He was a hell of a big help to me and I liked a lot of the things he did.

The big chance I got was on *Pinocchio* and it established me as a key animator. I gave the character a kind of fresh start. Everyone else had been fooling around with a puppet idea so much in mind, and I was a little outspoken about it. Ham Luske suggested I do a scene, and I did a little underwater scene where Pinocchio had the jackass ears and a long tail with a rock tied to it to keep him on the bottom, and he knocked on an oyster's shell, and when the shell opened, he tipped his hat and said, 'Pardon me, Pearl, but could you tell me where I could find Monstro the whale?'

I took the approach that I just forgot he was a puppet and did a cute little boy. I figured we could always make him into a puppet later – and this conception caught on with Walt. So I supervised the character through the rest of the picture. It really wasn't a promotion. It sort of took care of itself.

My favourite animation quote. Milt said this in 1976 and I've had it framed on many walls since:

QUOTATION FROM MILT KAHL 1976

It's a very difficult medium. Animation necessarily requires a pretty good draftsman, because you've got to turn things, to be able to draw well enough to turn things at every angle. You have to understand movement, which in itself is quite a study. You have to be an actor. You have to put on a performance, to be a showman, to be able to evaluate how good the entertainment is. You have to know what's the best way of doing it, and have an appreciation of where it belongs in the picture. You have to be a pretty good story man. To be a really good animator, then, you have to be a jack-of-all-trades. I don't mean to say that I'm all these things, but I try hard. I got accused over the years of being a fine draftsman. Actually, I don't really draw that well. It's just that I don't stop trying as quickly. I keep at it. I happen to have high standards and I try to meet them. I have to struggle like hell to make a drawing look good.

Milt said:

Walt was a fountain of ideas. They flowed out of him. A lot of them were rotten, you know. I remember one time we were having a meeting on *Jungle Book* and he comes up with this stupid thing. He said, 'You know what could happen? Mowgli grows up. And he gets into his teens, and adolescence, and then he's lured by civilisation – away from the jungle.' And I said, 'Yeah, the title could be *The Call of the Tame.*' He gave me a dirty look and just kept on talking. That's the relationship I had with him.

I never showed him a caricature of himself and I don't know if anybody else ever did. But he could probably laugh at himself, you know, he was a nice guy. Walt was eight years older than I. He was the boss and we treated him accordingly. But we could disagree. What was he gonna do? Fire me? It was a funny relationship I had with him though. It was kind of, as you say, adversarial. It was very amusing, actually. But that's the relationship I had with him.

The way Walt used me was to scatter me throughout the picture. I did a little of everything. I'd start a character off – and do enough footage to put it on the screen and establish it to the point where Walt could look at it and say, 'Well, yeah, that's great – that's what we want. That's the character.' And he was kidding himself, because that was not the character he was going to get at *all*. Because you were going to get a lot of these other people doing the thing for the picture – maybe three or four other animators. And I looked at their stuff – and I would have done it entirely differently.

Like *Alice in Wonderland*. I did some scenes there with the caterpillar where he says, 'And *who* – are *you*?' – and blows the smoke rings. Now that's a cute little Alice. But she didn't turn out that way in the picture. Anyway, I'd do a couple of hundred feet, two minutes or so – enough to start the characters off and then I'd move on to something else. And then other people would take over with varying degrees of ineptitude. It was frustrating for me because I could never look at a picture afterwards and say 'I did *this* and I did *that*' – because I *didn't*. I'd made a little part of it. I'd done enough to start the thing off and get it going. I would have enjoyed my work a lot more if I had been able to be concerned with one particular character, but I always had to scatter myself and be involved with all the characters – or pretty near all of them.

Some of the guys, like Frank, or Ollie or Ward – these guys would have a character and they'd get to do *everything* on this character. Like Ward did all of the mean goddamn cat in *Cinderella*. It's clever as all hell. But I could never get to do something like that. The closest I ever came to doing a character all the way through a picture – except for Medusa in *The Rescuers* – was Shere Khan in *The Jungle Book*. I did all of him except some stuff in the fight. Well, I didn't just do Shere Khan – I got the boy started, did a great deal of footage on the boy, Bagheera, the Snake and King Louie. Baloo, I did a little bit of – but Ollie Johnston did the main bulk of Baloo.

I was sort of left alone. When I had a sequence to do, or a character to do, they accepted what I had to do. I had quite a free rein in what I had to do with it.

It seems obvious to me that Walt Disney had Milt spreading himself through the pictures establishing characters and performances to set a standard and hold things together.

Milt said:

With Walt you had the understanding that you were going to be anonymous and we weren't really. We got good screen credit and stuff like that. I certainly never resented it. I got mad at him sometimes and would say, 'Well, you're so goddamned busy being a celebrity now, you can't come to meetings', and that sort of thing. That was when Walt was all interested in the Disneyland park.

Do you know about the anonymous notes thing? It started in a meeting on *Sleeping Beauty*. This is in 1955 when – just about the time the park opened – we couldn't get him in on meetings on the picture. We worked on this boy-meets-girl sequence for an awfully long time, and the overhead was mounting, and when somebody didn't know what the hell to charge something to, for his time – well, he'd charge it to *Sleeping Beauty*. It was a handy number.

So anyway, we couldn't get Walt in on the meetings – and *finally* we did. We got him in on a story meeting – on the same damn sequence – and, right at the end, when we were wrapping up the sequence, I said, 'Hey Walt, you're going to get this damn story going now, aren't you?' And he took that as personal criticism, and he said, 'Do you know how much footage we're turning out around here while you sons-of-bitches are working on this thing?' And he started telling me all the stuff they've done, and here we are all bogged down. And he bawled the hell out of the whole meeting. There were about seven or eight of us in there – and Walt rose from his seat to end the meeting. He started to leave the room, held the door open like he was going to go out in the hall, and got back to me again, and said, 'You overbearing bastard, I've got an – anon – anonymous note *thanking* me for telling you off!' And he slammed the door.

So I got down to my room and I sent him a message – 'Dear Walt, thanks for telling that overbearing bastard off. It did my heart good.' And I signed it 'Amomynum Anomynum' and I crossed it out about four times and ended with 'Anonymous'. I got a message back about two hours later in the middle of the afternoon. 'Dear Anonymous, do you know the difference between an executive producer and a vulture? Well, the difference is this: the vulture always waits till the guy's dead before he eats his ass out.'

So anyway, that started it off. I could write him anonymous notes and I could insult him all I wanted and he knew who they were from – and I always signed them 'Anonymous'. And he'd come back at me, 'Dear Anonymous'. It was a nice relationship, because the guy just could fly down your throat – and the next minute everything would be fine. He wouldn't stay mad at you, unless you were some guy he really didn't like.

I'm just as tough myself. I'm a hard taskmaster. I think if you set standards and other people don't meet them, then you're tough – and I think that's what happened. Walt was never unreasonable. I guess that's the best way to put it.

The trouble is that Walt had to go and die on us. We missed him terribly. Walt had, on the whole, damned excellent taste, and he understood the public. Don't ever sell

Walt short. We're just carrying something on here. None of us would ever have been able to work in this medium the way we do, except for Walt. I really loved that man – he was really a wonderful person.

I know that Milt had his scenes so thoroughly thought out that he rarely ever needed to shoot more than one pencil test. He told me, 'I don't have to look at the test. I know what it looks like. I *did* it. I wait and then I look at a bunch of the scenes cut together in continuity – so I can see how it's getting *over*.'

I asked Milt, 'How did you ever get that good?' His answer: 'Well, I *do* it a lot. And I *think* about it a lot.' He paused a while and said:

An analogy to that is the man who told this budding writer that writing is awfully easy. All you had to do is get a pencil, a typewriter or anything, and just put down whatever occurred to you. But the rub is that it's the *occurring* that's difficult. So that's the way it is. I think the conception is always the thing – and the amount of work – and the amount of *thought* you put into it.

Anyway, I think my main asset is the fact that I didn't have any limitations. That's what separated me from the other guys. There are a lot of guys who are only good at certain things. I think a guy ought to be good at anything. I wouldn't allow myself any limitations. I could do stuff that others could do and I could do it better than they did. And I'm getting better all the time. That's why everybody says I'm so modest and self-effacing . . .

When we were younger, we'd try to have a lot of fun with everything we did. I suppose there was a lot of competition between the animators, but we never felt that. We made a habit of helping each other, and talking over our business with other animators too.

I said to Milt, 'But according to your assistant, all the other animators came to your door, hungry for drawings, and used to come in cap-in-hand, and continually disturb you, and say, "How do I do this?"'

Milt replied:

I had an awful lot of that. People's assistants would come in, and I'd end up being a clean-up man, make good drawings for them. But I felt it was my job, though I'd bitch about it an awful lot. I'm probably selfish; all I care about is my own work. It has to be true, because I really don't care too much, you know, it's selfish. But I did spend a lot of my time helping people.

We're all in this thing together. And it's really hard to give anyone the credit or the blame for anything. To give all the credit to the animators is as ridiculous as if you gave all of the credit for the success of live action pictures to the actors. So it's that old group effort thing. It takes a lot of people.

When I first saw Milt's drawings on his desk, I was struck by how different and more sophisticated they were from the usual Disney 'look'. 'My God,' I said, 'now I see what these things are supposed to look like. This is the original! Everybody's copying you – but not so well.'

Milt said, 'When it leaves my desk, gravity gets it.'

Milt's signature looks like a fishing fly. Fly fishing demands a delicacy as well as a sure touch, which was what appealed to Milt throughout his life. He triumphed in writing 'Milt' with his line on a long cast – and placing his bug or fly on the spot.

I said to Milt: 'It seems to me that apart from Ub Iwerks's early work in the 20s, there are three architects of what I think is the Disney style. One is Albert Hurter; his work in the 1930s seemed to have a big influence.' Milt agreed. 'Yes.' 'And then Freddie Moore with his charming drawings – certainly in his early work before he hit the bottle – and that goes up to 1943 or so.' Milt nodded. 'Yes.' I said, 'And then it goes right over to you. The look of everything from then on is your drawings.'

Milt answered:

Well, yes, that's very flattering. The only thing is, though, that you have to remember that all the way through it was always a group effort. I probably had more to do with it than most of the people did, because I helped more people in drawing. What I object to is people singling me out, singling out my animation as being maybe better because I was a better draughtsman. I think that's sort of cheapening it. It's selling it short because it's not the draughtsmanship – it's the *conception*.

Although he worked virtually all his life with Walt Disney, you only have to look at Milt's work to realise that he made animation his own medium. Anything he could conceive of, he could execute – with an elegance and perception which is stunning to the layman and top exponent alike.

Milt said: 'I have high standards. If you don't have something to aspire to, what have you got? You have to have high standards. I think that's part of any profession. If you don't aim high, you're not going to get anywhere. I always figured that was the way you operate.'

12/30

DEAR DICK:
   IT TAKES A PRETTY GOOD PROD TO
GET ME OFF MY ASS WITH MY CORRES-
PONDENCE, AND I'VE JUST HAD ONE, WHICH
NOT ONLY GOT ME TO WRITING, BUT EVEN
GOT ME ON THE PHONE, ONLY TO FIND YOU
WERE IN NEW YORK.
   WE SAW YOUR EPIC ON THE 21ST AND
THOUGHT IT WAS SIMPLY WONDERFUL,
ORIGINAL, FRESH AND BEAUTIFULLY CONCEIVED.
EVERYONE HERE WHO HAS SEEN IT IS VERY
MUCH IMPRESSED, AND I PERSONALLY AM
OVERWHELMED, PARTICULARLY CONSIDERING
THE TIME ELEMENT AND THE PEOPLE YOU
HAD TO USE.

Here's an example of Milt's encouragement. We'd just finished *A Christmas Carol*.
This was early on, before I started to really get it all together.

Everyone said Milt was the closest thing to a human camera that you could ever get. He said, 'I'm in the habit of studying the action in anything I see – and figuring out why things move as they do. I always try to figure out the mechanics of it. I think it becomes second nature to you. But it's not the most important thing – the play's the thing.'

Once I asked for a basic animation rule of some sort, and the answer came – 'Well, you need at least five drawings to bring something in or take something out of the screen.' 'What?' Later I was shooting some live action of my 5-year-old daughter, Claire, for a film. She was running up steps and on one take she slipped and fell down out of the scope frame. Back in the cutting room – 'Stop the machine!' I counted the frames as she fell out of shot. Five.

I rang Milt up after some years' gap and said, 'I've had a rough time for a while and haven't felt like phoning.'

I said, 'How are you?' He said, 'Not so good, you know, I'm getting kind of old.' I said, 'Come on, you're only about 67.' He said, 'I'm 76.' 'What?' I gasped. 'Look, I'll be right there . . .' I'd always be telling him that I was starting to get it all together. He'd say, 'Then *show* me.' So I wanted to screen for him twenty completed minutes of my epic *The Thief and the Cobbler* in order to show him that I finally knew my onions and could handle everything. Milt was in Marin County outside San Francisco, so I booked Industrial Light & Magic's Theatre (where we coincidentally later composited *Roger Rabbit*) to show the film, and jumped on a plane.

We were in this big pink ILM viewing theatre after they'd finished a day dubbing *Ewoks* – just me, Milt and his wife Julie, in the front row. After my film finished, both the projectionist and the sound man came running out of their booths and said, 'That's the greatest animated film we've ever seen! Did *you* do that?'

'Yes.'

'Wow! You must be the world's greatest animator!'

'No!' I jumped up and made a big theatrical gesture at Milt. '*This* is the world's greatest animator!'

Afterwards I asked Milt, 'Any criticisms?' Pause.

'Yes. When you shot that thief out of the giant catapult, you needed more frames to go out.'

I fell around laughing. 'Well, we *had* five frames at first and it was too slow – and I kept cutting it down for impact to four and three and two – and ended up with one long cinemascope blur for one frame.' We had quite an argument.

I'm so lucky to have known this man who had the built-in artist's standards and who just kept getting better and better until he decided to stop. He gave me such help, although he always said, 'Hell, Dick, you aren't getting any help.' I didn't know him that deeply at all – we were just very friendly over a long period. But I felt and still feel such a strong connection with him because of what he stood for – excellence for its own sake – and because he spared nothing in pursuit of it, and actually achieved it consistently.

In what turned out to be the farewell interview I did with him, I asked him, 'Could you say simply what it is that you do or did all those years?'

Milt said:

Well, I just had an awful lot of fun with the medium, that's all. Working with Walt and being part of that operation was pretty damn good. It was quite a privilege. Anyway, I did all my developing in the goddamn medium. All my artistic development was at the Disney studio.

I had a kind of instinct for what would be the right thing. That's the only way I can explain it. You just seem to understand what the problem calls for, you know.

It just turned out that it was an ideal medium for me. It really was.

Last known photo of Milt. He's at his favourite table at his favourite restaurant. He tipped the waiters so much, they practically lay down as carpeting. 'Oh, Sir, Sir!'

I'M BACK!
From coffee. Stan Green, Milt's
assistant, found this on his desk.

THE THIEF AND THE COBBLER: **IN PRODUCTION**

Working on the camel scene

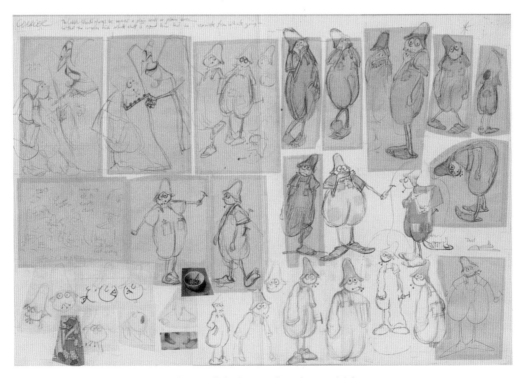

Early model sheets for the Cobbler

Caricature of Art and Ken while I draw the Thief

SIR FELIX AYLMER   5th JUNE 1974   R williams

Thief roughs

With Vincent Price as Zigzag the Grand Vizier

With Mo working on *The Thief and the Cobbler*

Drawing Yumyum

The cutting room

Route sheet meeting

Flipping drawings

A note from Imogen Sutton:

From the beginning Dick and I agreed *Adventures in Animation* would be a joint venture. Dick's illness and subsequent death meant I had to complete the book we'd started together and tell parts of the story he'd been unable to finish. In the following pages, I've indicated where the text is Dick's own words.

THE THIEF AND THE COBBLER: **AN ENDING?**

On 13 May 1992, in the City of London, a lawyer declared:

'Mr Williams, *The Thief and the Cobbler* is no longer yours.'

After twenty years' labour on what Dick considered the culmination of his life's work, the film met an abrupt end.

We climbed into a taxi and looked at each other. Dick said, 'Well, that's an elephant off my back.' And we both laughed.

We went back to the studio in Camden where animators, background artists, painters and tracers were still working away. Soon after, we announced that in two weeks the studio would shut, that all the artwork and film would be packed away and that the film would be finished elsewhere. We knew some of the crew had already been offered jobs on finishing it. We gave our blessing to anyone who wanted to do that. Gradually, everything disappeared – packed, shipped, gone.

On our last day in the studio, when nothing was left, our 3-year-old daughter ran across the vast empty space and found the precise spot where Dick's desk used to be. She then proceeded to sing and dance in a circle as though his desk was still there.

* * *

How did we get to this point?

Who Framed Roger Rabbit (1988) had been a huge success. It did something new – it mixed live action and animation and made both worlds credible. After the premiere at Radio City Music Hall in New York, we headed to Cape Cod where I was making a film on Simone de Beauvoir. I was going to film an interview with Marge Piercy, the novelist and poet, who was a lifelong fan of the writer. I worked during the day and in the evenings we went to the local cinema to see whatever was on. After three nights, we'd run out of films to view so we decided to watch *Roger Rabbit* with a regular audience and see how they responded. The cinema was full and their reactions were audible – in particular, to the scene where the Rabbit is about to be plunged into a chemical mix deadly to cartoon characters known as 'the dip'.

As the credits ran up the screen, we got up to go but the family in front of us remained seated. I overheard the father say, 'Let's not leave, there's something I want to see.' Curious, I pulled Dick back down and pointed my finger at the people in front.

As Dick's credit came on the screen as Director of Animation, the man said, 'Boy, he must have had a helluva job,' and got up to leave. I said to Dick, 'You must tell him it's you.' He was reluctant, but as the family went down the aisle he tapped the man on the shoulder and said, 'I'm Richard Williams, I directed the animation.' The man pulled his daughter close to his body, as though protecting her from a madman. 'It's true,' said Dick, turning around to show him the back of his special crew jacket, which had *Who Framed Roger Rabbit* written across it. He turned back and the man held out his hand to shake Dick's. 'Welcome to Wellfleet,' he said. That was it – nothing more was said and they left the cinema ahead of us.

Dick thought this was the best of all the reactions to the film.

Its success gave him the credibility to finally complete *The Thief and the Cobbler* – a film he'd been working on for over twenty years, using the money from his commercial work to employ the 'old guys', like Ken Harris and Art Babbitt, to animate sequences including the film's complex battle sequence. Dick had prioritised this sequence because he thought no one else would want to take the time or money to do it properly.

The story of *The Thief and the Cobbler* was like an *Arabian Nights* tale and its design was inspired by Persian miniatures. The story is set in a magical Golden City. Its hero is a young, simple cobbler who finds himself up against a thief who will stop at nothing to steal anything, including the three golden balls that sit atop a golden minaret. Legend has it that if the balls are ever taken away the city will be destroyed. Meanwhile, a huge army with a diabolical war machine is assembling to invade. The Cobbler leaves the city with its princess to discover the secret of how to save it from the invaders but, in the end, it is the simplest of things which does the job – the tack the Cobbler uses to mend shoes.

Who Framed Roger Rabbit brought Dick two Oscars in 1989. This provided the springboard to finance the finishing of *The Thief and the Cobbler*. Warner Bros. would distribute it, Fuji Bank were to provide the funds and the Completion Bond Company would guarantee that it got finished. By 1990 the film was underway in a large studio in Camden, London.

We doubled up the main office as a screening room – and everyone would crowd in to see the latest rushes. Dick couldn't believe it – it was the most exciting time of his life, seeing what was being created daily by an enthusiastic and hard-working crew.

So why did it come to a crashing end? Like many accidents, it wasn't just one thing – it was several coming together. The film had its already low budget shaved at the last minute to push it over the line. We were promised there would be more money eventually but that didn't happen. The pace of the work was extraordinary but it wasn't good enough for the Completion Bond Company and they decided to step in and directed Dick to do a storyboard to fill the gaps that hadn't been animated.

He'd always resisted doing a complete storyboard but now hc happily got on with doing what was necessary. Then came the next element in the crash – Japanese banks were going through a rough time and were calling in all their loans. Fuji Bank was no exception. Warner Bros. got nervous and asked to see a rough cut of the film. We flew out to Los Angeles so we could discuss how to proceed.

Warners viewed the film – it didn't make sense, they said, and so they decided to pull out. We discovered very quickly that the projectionist had forgotten to screen one of the reels. Of course it didn't make sense. We tried to explain, asked if we could run the film again for them, but it was over. They refused to meet with us – a Warner executive explained in a fax, 'Nothing personal, just business.'

Two weeks later we were called into a crystal skyscraper filled with lawyers and the film was taken away from Dick.

Over the years, versions of the film came out, finished off in different countries, released in different forms. The two main characters in Dick's film were silent – in one of the versions, they had been given voices and songs had been added. Dick was advised never to see the botched film – or he'd jump off a bridge.

* * *

Several things happened very quickly. It was clear that staying around in London would be grim. I counselled silence. 'Let's stay schtum,' I said, 'and get out of here.'

By chance, some months earlier, when the film had been going well, we'd been talking about what we'd do when it was finished. We liked the idea of living somewhere else. Dick had loved New Mexico when we had visited Emery Hawkins. There were big skies and it would be completely new. I favoured British Columbia, which I'd visited as a child. We were told there was an island called Salt Spring which was just like 'sparkling water'.

Both Dick and I had lived on islands – he on Ibiza in the 1950s, and I on Ovalau in Fiji in the 1960s. We liked the idea of an island. Somewhat crazily, when there was a long weekend break from the film, we left our daughter with a friend and took off to British Columbia for a couple of days. Arriving in Vancouver Airport, we were asked to show our return tickets, and when it became clear we were there for only two days it was assumed we were drug runners. Taken into a small office, we were cross-questioned about why we were there just for the weekend; we tried to explain, but they weren't listening. Eventually, I said in a stern voice, 'Look, I know it might not look like it – but we're film producers – my husband has three Oscars.' This startled the immigration officers and we were let through.

We travelled on a night ferry from Vancouver through the Gulf Islands. Although we were exhausted from the flight, we were entranced. It was so quiet and because the sky was completely black – no light pollution – you could see all the stars.

Oddly, although Dick had got as far as the Rockies when he was a student, he'd never been to British Columbia. He was hooked before it was even daylight. Driving around the island, he couldn't get over the size of the trees – so much taller than in Ontario. We stopped at various realtors, got details of houses and fax numbers for the future. We were ready to move there when the film was finished.

This meant that when we knew we had to get out of London quickly, we already had a plan – we'd go to Salt Spring Island. We faxed the realtors and they faxed us back fuzzy pictures of houses. 'That's it,' said Dick, 'that's the one.' It was a blurred image of what looked like a large treehouse set among grand trees.

We phoned the realtor and said we were coming out to get the house. He was astonished. So only six weeks after the lawyers' meeting which ended so many years of Dick's animation work, we were on our way to a new life on an island in the Pacific Northwest.

A NEW LIFE

For Dick, being in Canada meant being a student. He'd left the Ontario College of Art without graduating and, returning home after forty years, he became a student again. Very quickly he hooked up with the music scene on the island and began playing his cornet several times a week – including in a big band. Through this, he met a musician who also taught arranging. A small group was formed and Dick began taking lessons and arranging his own jazz pieces. He found a life drawing class and this became a weekly event. Occasionally, other things emerged. A retired surgeon taught anatomy for artists – Dick filled books with anatomy drawings; he quickly learned the terms and could name many muscles.

All of this happened very quickly. We had made such a huge change in our lives that all the recent troubles disappeared from view and, apart from odd legal letters, we were undisturbed. We gave our phone number to very few people and when a journalist discovered it and rang up, I was able to change the number the same afternoon. We had found a peaceful place where Dick could take the time to do things he previously hadn't had time for. He relished studying. He wasn't retiring – far from it, he was busier than ever, sharpening up his skills and craft.

* * *

Our life on the island settled into an easy pattern. One of us dropped our daughter off at the 'Little Red School House' each morning – a beautiful drive through woodland. Dick then disappeared to his garage studio, and I began work on a novel set on the island. We had recovered from the trauma of the film very quickly – we were happily out of that world. But one day, when we were looking at our finances, it became clear we had to start earning again. We were sat at our kitchen table overlooking the Pacific. The conversation ceased as we both became thoughtful – what could we do, living on an island off the west coast of Canada? There was no internet then – no email, no mobile phones, we only had a fax machine and a landline.

I spoke up first, 'This is the age of information and you've got the information.'

Dick immediately responded, 'Let's do something with that.'

This was the start of our masterclasses, which Dick named *The Animator's Survival Kit*.

A few years before, we'd been to a couple of screenwriting masterclasses and decided to use their three-day formula. It would be a Friday, Saturday and Sunday – so animators would only have to take one day off work. We would design the masterclasses for maximum impact – start with glamour by screening clips of Dick's work, cover the basics, and then gradually build up to the 'sophisticated use of the basics'. The question then became – where would we do a practice run of this idea? The obvious location was Vancouver. It was only a ferry ride away and it was known as a film centre and had plenty of screening facilities. We decided we needed a good screening room to show clips and a stage in front where Dick could talk, draw and act things out. We'd provide plenty of coffee and cookies and suggest places for a quick lunch in the break. We wanted it to be informative, fun, and to allow time for chat between sessions.

An art-house cinema perfectly fitted the bill. We guessed at numbers and did some sums. Twenty-five attendees would mean we'd lose money; thirty, we'd break even; anything over thirty-five, we'd begin to make some money.

The next question was how to advertise. There was no internet – the usual approach then was to advertise in trade magazines and hand out leaflets at a relevant event. There was a film festival coming up in Vancouver and it prompted us to reserve a date for the masterclass, firm up the three-day programme, get leaflets made and adverts booked. It felt as though we were leaping into the unknown, but it was perfect work for me as we now had two small children and I could fit it into domestic gaps.

Dick was the front-man – and so obviously couldn't appear in person to sell our event – so it was I who went to Vancouver to distribute leaflets at the film festival. I stood outside screenings and waited for everyone to come out, handing out leaflets to those who would accept them. I felt like a billboard woman – most people completely ignored me and the few who took leaflets quickly dumped them into a nearby waste bin.

However, in one brief moment things turned around. I stepped into a lift and there was a young man wearing a jacket that read 'Warner Bros. Animation'. I'd heard Warner Bros., well known for their short films, had decided to make their first animated feature film.

'How about that,' I said to the young man, 'you're just the person I was looking for.'

The young man looked startled but then quickly intrigued by what I began talking about – an animation class with Richard Williams. 'I think my boss would be interested in this,' he said. It turned out his boss was Max Howard, who had worked on the management side of production on *Who Framed Roger Rabbit*. Max wasn't interested in a Vancouver masterclass but was interested in the feasibility of an 'in-house' class at Warner Bros. We hadn't actually done one masterclass yet, but I merrily agreed this was possible.

* * *

By now the few ads I'd taken out in trade magazines were getting responses. I'd deliberately put the fax/answer machine in our woodshed so I didn't have to hear it ringing or whirring. Every now and then I'd go and check on it and, gradually but steadily, there were more and more enquiries about the masterclass. Attendees filled out a form with their details and numbers began to rise. We reached break-even point quickly and then, gradually, hit the point where we'd make some money – in the end the total number of attendees was forty-six. We were delighted.

* * *

We'd heard of Pixar, but were surprised when a group booking came in for thirteen Pixar animators. Why would CG animators want to sign up with a classical, hand-drawn animator like Dick? It was a question he asked them on day one of the masterclass. 'What can you guys have to learn from me?' he said. 'Wait and see,' they said. 'We'll let you know at the end of the class.'

It turned out they'd just wrapped the first *Toy Story* and a Canadian friend had told them about the masterclass. 'Let's go and see what Williams has to say,' they decided. They came with no expectations, sat through the three-day class and at the end answered Dick's question about what they had to learn from him: '95 per cent of what you're teaching is relevant to us,' they said. 'It's the principles of animation that we can use too.'

The Pixar animators wrote to us after the class: 'We came back with our brains on fire to apply the techniques and timings you presented in our work.' They invited us down to their studio in Emeryville, California, and, after showing us around, offered to have Dick stay for three months so they could teach him how to animate on a computer. It was a generous offer, but Dick knew he was a draughtsman and hand-drawn animation was where he'd remain. However, the meeting with the Pixar animators became a turning point for us. Animation was booming and with the success of *Toy Story*, computer-generated animation was taking off everywhere. This meant we had a market. We'd learned that what Dick was teaching was relevant to all forms of animation – classical, computer, games and stop motion.

Over the next five years we gave twenty-three masterclasses around the world – in San Francisco, Los Angeles, New York, London, Sydney, Hong Kong, Annecy, at the European Film School and as in-house events at Warner Bros., Will Vinton Studios and Blue Sky Studios.

The masterclass at the Annecy International Animation Festival

The participants came from all over the world; studios would send people across continents to attend. Because of the numbers, we ended up doing two masterclasses in San Francisco. I noticed one participant had signed up for both. 'Why did you do that?' I asked, after his second class. 'I took notes in the first class,' he said, 'and in the second I just wanted to draw what Richard was doing.'

As everyone was taking notes and copying Dick's drawings, it became clear we had to consider doing a book. The structure would be based on the masterclasses, but there would be many more examples. Dick was clear – this was not to be a coffee-table book. It was to be a useful book, a work book, a book he'd have loved to have had beside his desk. He knew that most animators aren't great book readers and so it had to be accessible – that's why most of it was handwritten in Dick's characteristic print.

In 1997 we moved back to the UK and, for a while, lived in Oxford. This was when work on the book really got under way. With some finished pages, we approached a publisher of art books and were immediately made an offer. 'But you'll have to get rid of the handwriting,' they said, 'We can't do foreign editions with your handwriting.' Dick was adamant; animators would respond to handwriting, but not to printed text. It was then that I approached Faber, renowned for their film books. Walter Donohue, the film editor, understood the handwriting aspect immediately. 'I see,' he said, 'it's a work book.'

So that was it. We had a publisher and Dick was now writing the book full-time between masterclasses. We'd moved to Pembrokeshire in Wales and converted part of a barn into a studio. It was here Dick slowly but steadily wrote, drew and designed the pages of the book. We had a deadline; Dick worked out how many pages he had to do each day to meet it. Every evening at supper our son would ask, 'How many pages did you do today?' Often, not enough.

Because of the unusual way in which the book was being produced – as camera-ready pages – it meant that its production could carry on as the pages were being written. Towards the end of the schedule, every Monday morning we'd drop the kids at school and I'd get on the train with whatever pages Dick had finished that week and deliver them to Faber in London. It was a five-hour trip each way and I couldn't get back the same day. At the very end, the boundaries of the schedule had been stretched to breaking point – we had agreed a date with Faber for the last delivery of pages.

It was the final Monday morning and Dick had worked all night – but he still had a complex double-page spread to do. It would take him twenty-four hours. Rather than delay delivery of everything, I suggested I go up to London anyway with what was finished and he could send the final two pages the next day by Special Delivery.

Faber weren't happy when I said that there were two pages outstanding but that they'd definitely be there on Wednesday. On Tuesday morning, Dick rang me to say he'd just delivered the last pages to the post office and was about to go to a café and have eggs on toast. The relief in his voice made me quiver. I found myself in a state of shock – it was done.

The Animator's Survival Kit was first published in the UK in hardback and paperback in 2001 and in the US in 2002. In the end, developments in digital technology meant that

Dick's handwriting was no bar to foreign editions and soon after there were editions in nine languages.

* * *

While we continued doing masterclasses, I thought we needed to film one of them – if only as a record. But where? We'd met Chris Wedge when he came to a masterclass in San Francisco. He was one of the founders of Blue Sky Studios, based just outside New York City. I wrote to him and explained we were planning to do two masterclasses in New York, and asked if would he be interested in us doing a filmed 'in-house' masterclass at Blue Sky afterwards. He enthusiastically agreed, and I began planning the film production side of it. We'd need three cameras, and an extra day for the masterclass as the filming might slow it up – so we decided on four days. It was 1997, and we used the top-of-the-range Sony format available then; as we were in the US, it was shot on the NTSC American broadcast system. The filming went well although on the last day, as we broke for lunch, a summer shower came belting down. It was only then that I discovered the building had a tin roof! The noise was shattering. Potentially, it could have ruined the rest of the filming. Amazingly, the shower lasted for just the lunch hour and then stopped. It was a lesson for me – before filming always ask what the roof is made of.

* * *

The video cassettes were popped into boxes and shipped to our home in Wales. Ten years later we opened them. The book had been out for seven years and was doing well – wasn't it time to take a look at the video material and see what we could do with it? We initially imported editing equipment to cut the material in the Welsh barn, but it was obvious we needed something longer term. We'd met Peter Lord and David Sproxton of Aardman Animations and wondered if they might be able to help. I arranged to meet Peter at their studio on the outskirts of Bristol. They had an edit suite we could rent and an extra room in which to put Dick's rostrum camera. It had become clear very quickly that we'd need to animate sequences to pop into the live action material of Dick teaching. It was also clear we'd need a title sequence – the obvious choice was to animate the figures Dick had put on the cover of the book. Knowing this wasn't a simple job, I suggested Dick start on that first. With the help of animator Neil Boyle, compositor Pieter Van Houte and editor Don Fairservice, the project got under way. Nine months later we had a title sequence.

The way the film was originally shot became crucial ten years on. It was on what was now an old-fashioned video format – as well as being on the NTSC system. This created real complexity in how we were going to put it all together and produce DVDs that would work worldwide. The first meeting to work out technicalities took place at our post-production house Films@59, headed by their project manager Bridget Blythe and Tom Barnes, Technical Director at Aardman. There were thirteen people at the meeting. We never met like that again, but over the two years of production everyone knew what they had to do and each deadline was met. In going through the rushes and looking at the structure of the book, we decided on a sixteen-DVD box set. I was worried that if we left all the post-production to the end, we might have some slippage in the schedule – so we decided to do the editing of the live action sequences, the inserting of the animated ones and the post-production in batches of three to four DVDs.

It was time to move again. We wanted to live as well as work in Bristol and put our Welsh house on the market. Unfortunately, the banking crisis hit in 2008 and we found ourselves renting in Bristol while trying to sell our home. Dick loved animating in his barn, so we commuted up and down the M4 as I stayed to edit in Bristol.

One lunchtime Dick rang me in the cutting room to say he was feeling unwell. He thought he needed to get to a hospital. He wanted to come to Bristol. I offered to order a taxi but he insisted on driving. He sounded dreadful and I rushed back to our rental house to wait for him. He got out of the car very slowly. We set off for the hospital, which was ten minutes' walk away, but at the end of the street he said he'd like to take a taxi.

Various tests were done and we were shocked when we were told he'd had a heart attack. He would need a triple bypass operation. Following the operation, he became very ill and was put on a life support machine. I had to make a decision about the DVD project – could we continue? Don had editing he could get on with and Neil was busy animating. 'Carry on,' I said, 'Let's see how Dick does.'

Dick slowly made his way to 'the exit' – as he put it – and left hospital in early 2009. He spent one week reading the papers and then couldn't stand it. He had to work. So he found an easy sequence to animate and got back at it. He started weekly rehabilitation classes at the hospital which involved building up strength in a highly monitored gym setting. I was amazed at what they had all the heart patients doing – and Dick was determined to get well. We went to St Ives for a few days to potter around and consider what to do. By the end of the short holiday, he had decided he would still work on the DVDs.

* * *

Dick animated in a corner of the cutting room as Don and I edited the footage. Neil and Pieter worked mainly at home, but would show up to plan the next sequence and finalise each batch of material. It took shape slowly but we didn't miss a beat. By the end of a two-year production period, the only thing that held us up – ridiculously – was the boxes to contain the DVDs. We had found a good sturdy type of box. The man we ordered the boxes through took the measurements and made a sample for us to take home. What a lovely box it was. It was hardly believable that after all this time we were actually going to have sixteen DVDs to put in it. I took some DVDs off the shelf – counted sixteen and popped them in. They slid around – it was obvious that the box was meant for seventeen DVDs. Thankfully, the mistake was caught in time, but it held everything up and we were a month later than planned with the first sales.

Box set of *The Animator's Survival Kit* DVDs

* * *

It was because we'd created over 400 animated sequences for the DVDs that the next project emerged. Apps were just becoming fashionable and Faber were interested in creating an iPad app from the book. Because we already had the animation, we thought it would be an easy transfer from the book to an app. It wasn't. Everything had to be redesigned for an iPad; technically popping in the animation and making it all flow was more complicated than we'd expected. Eoin Noble at Faber and the team at Agant made it work.

I'd been talking to the Academy of Motion Picture Arts and Sciences (AMPAS) about an exhibition of Dick's artwork, and the possibilities of interactivity with the iPad app created a framework. In 2013 the exhibition at the Wilshire Boulevard head office of AMPAS opened in Los Angeles. On opening night, in the vast auditorium, Dick gave the nineteenth Marc Davis Celebration of Animation lecture. It was two hours long with clips; he talked about the great animators he'd worked with and how they had influenced his work. Three months later the exhibition ended with a screening of *The Thief and the Cobbler: A Moment in Time.*

* * *

On 13 May 1992, when *The Thief and the Cobbler* was 'no longer yours, Mr Williams', we'd returned to the studio without initially saying anything to anyone. There were legal details to sort out before the news could be announced.

I went into the cutting room and asked the editor to make a 'slash' dupe of the film – both sound and picture – at my expense. A slash dupe is a copy of a film made in the lab overnight. The quality you get will vary according to the chemical 'bath' that night – it could be good, it could be terrible. It is always a risk.

The following morning there were twelve reels of film and twelve reels of sound waiting for me. I got into a taxi and took them to our London home. Weeks later, they were packed with our furniture and shipped to British Columbia where they joined the fax machine in the woodshed.

It was eight years later in Annecy, France, that we opened the cans.

* * *

Roy Disney, the son of Walt's brother Roy, had been bombarded over the years by keen animators asking him to 'save' *The Thief*. We'd heard these rumours but didn't think much of them until we found out that he was being made Honorary President at the Annecy Animation Festival in 2000. Coincidentally, we'd arranged to do a masterclass at the same time. Dick already knew Roy from *Roger Rabbit*.

This was an opportunity to see if it was possible to salvage *The Thief*.

I contacted the Annecy people and asked if there was a theatre in the town that could screen a film 'sepmag' – with sound and picture on separate reels.

No, there wasn't. But there was a screening room in Lyons which could. The difficulty was that Lyons was almost two hours' drive from Annecy. Would Roy want to take that time just to see the film? I contacted his office and suggested the plan. 'Roy would love to go to Lyons,' they said. 'It's the location of his favourite restaurant.'

After we finished the masterclass, we were all set to go to Lyons, where we had booked the screening room. We had imagined Roy would come with his wife Patty, but we were told there would be a group of them in two cars – including two French animation directors – the twin brothers Paul and Gaëtan Brizzi who were currently making a film at Disney – and Howard Green, Vice President, Studio Communications. As they were bringing a crew of people, we thought we should bring a crew – in our case our two children, aged 6 and 11, and our friend John Ferguson, a great double bass player who would keep an eye on the kids.

We arrived early at the location and were surprised to find that the theatre we'd hired was in what looked like a barn. It was at the bottom of a hill on top of which was an elegant house. We then discovered we'd landed at a historic site in film history – this was the place where one of the first shots of celluloid film was taken, of workers coming through the Lumière Factory's gates; above was the home of the Lumière brothers, now a museum. Henri was the projectionist, a charming man wearing white gloves as he handled the film. In my imperfect French I told him we were delighted he could run the picture and sound separately – but he then informed me that although he had two projectors for the picture, which meant those film reels would run smoothly one after the other, he only had one sound projector. This would mean a five-minute reel change after each sound reel. There were twelve reels and not only would this add considerable time to the screening, it would also disrupt the viewing of the film. We had no choice but to continue as planned.

We waited outside for the Disney group, expecting them to arrive as we had, down below. But, glancing upwards, we caught sight of them attempting to walk down the very steep, grass-covered hill from the museum. Because of the incline, they gradually sped up and were running. They arrived panting with excitement. 'Did you know this is the location of the beginning of cinema?' So before I could explain that our viewing was to be both disjointed and extended, everyone was taking photos of the old building.

Eventually, I did explain the technical problem but, in their enthusiasm for the location, the issue was brushed aside. Thus started the strangest viewing experience. We were all spread around the theatre – our children sat in front of us. The first reel started and ten minutes later stopped. Everyone began talking – astonished by what they were seeing. The next reel started – and then stopped. More animated chatter. So it went on. The film was ninety minutes long, plus an extra hour for the changeovers. Dick and I hadn't seen it since the studio had closed. It was exactly as it had been on 13 May 1992 – with finished sequences in full colour, drawn animation in pencil and Dick's storyboard frames. The soundtrack had all the voices, and rough sound mixes including music.

As the chatter continued between reels, Dick and I sat there transfixed. Despite being unfinished, the film was extraordinary. That was the reaction of the Disney team as well. To see a film with breaks every ten minutes was not an ideal way to view it – but somehow it had worked in our favour. Each break was a time for discussion, appreciation and anticipation for what was to come next. The film ended with a dramatic climax – the war machine sequence. The theatre went silent. It was more, much more than the audience had expected. As the lights came up, everyone remained silent for a few moments and then superlatives flew.

Our reaction was one of shock. Part of that was a reaction to the content of the film but also to its quality. When I'd asked for the 'slash dupe' to be made, I was taking a chance with what we'd get. We hadn't touched the film since then; we were only seeing this particular print for the first time. We knew that we'd been very lucky – the slash dupe was the best possible version of the work print. We couldn't have hoped for better. Our response to this viewing was delight mixed with relief. It had also sown ideas about how it might be possible to 'save' the film.

As the excitement subsided, the conversation turned to how late we were for the lunch reservation at Roy's favourite restaurant – Paul Bocuse. We piled into our three vans and set off across Lyons. It was 3 p.m. and the restaurant would normally have closed its doors by that time, but phone calls had been made and they had been told to expect us. As our convoy of cars pulled up, waiting outside, in full restaurant uniform, were the entire staff from chefs to waiters. We knew that this wasn't in our honour, but in Roy's. We were led into a private dining room, where it was made clear that the children were to have a separate table. John offered to sit with them.

The next question – for the Disney team but not us – was whether they should have a proper lunch or save themselves for a special banquet being put on for them by the Mayor of Annecy that evening. There was no argument. They would have a full Bocuse lunch.

Several hours later we stumbled out. We waved the Disney crew off, clambered into our car and spent the journey in a state of stunned disbelief. What a day it had been. Almost inevitably, there had been talk of how Disney's might finish the film properly and how that conversation must be kept going.

But the biggest results for us were our rediscovery of how magnificent the film was, and that it held up despite being unfinished, and our realisation that the print we had was surprisingly good.

* * *

There were conversations with Roy over a number of years. He and Patty invited us to their Irish castle and told us they'd dreamed about the film for weeks after the screening. Contracts were sent – but with caveats about who had creative control. Roy even visited us in Wales, flying into a tiny local airport.

It was an extended period of discussion but nothing came of it. Coming out of a doorway in Ireland, Roy and I were very close together. I said quietly, 'You know it doesn't matter, Roy.' He looked quite shocked. But for us, it didn't. If we were to finish the film, it had to be on exactly the right terms. Having lost the film once already, it would otherwise be meaningless.

We met up with Roy for a final time at the Disney studio in LA. The dialogue was still going on but nothing had happened. Dick spoke frankly to Roy on that last occasion. They were both in their seventies: 'One of us will die before this gets done,' said Dick.

* * *

So how were we able to screen *The Thief and the Cobbler: A Moment in Time* at AMPAS in 2013?

It was the age of digitisation and because we'd seen the film at the screening in Lyons and found that the slash dupe was in good condition, we decided there was something we could do. In 2012 I went to LA and met with Randy Haberkamp, the Managing Director of Preservation and Foundation Programs at AMPAS. I asked if they would be interested in supporting the reconstruction of the film and in an exhibition of Dick's artwork, including the forthcoming iPad app. He was interested and supported both projects.

Our goal was to preserve the film as it had been on the day it was taken away. It was digitised and we booked a few days of film grading with Max Horton to improve the colour balance, and with Adrian Rhodes to give us a more complete sound mix.

Obviously, the film was not finished, but the idea was that an audience would be taken behind the scenes – rather like a rehearsal of an opera where some of the cast are in costume and others aren't. It would be the exact same film as our rough cut on the day we lost it, with a little polish to help the colour and sound. We called the final result *The Thief and the Cobbler: A Moment in Time* because it describes exactly what it is.

* * *

The Academy went further with their support. Soon after the exhibition in Hollywood, I received a phone call out of the blue from a lawyer representing a distribution company. His voice was angry and demanding: 'We can no longer keep paying for the storage of your artwork from the film *The Thief and the Cobbler*. What are you going to do about it?'

I was happy to tell him the artwork from the film hadn't been my responsibility since 1992. However, I had an idea about who might be interested in resolving his problem. I contacted Randy and told him about it. The artwork was in a warehouse and took up a vast amount of space. Much of it was not from the original film, but from the various versions of it produced and distributed after 1992. The Academy – helped by funding from ASIFA-Hollywood – took possession of the artwork, curated it, plucked out the original material and saved the collection.

It took over twenty years but both the film and the artwork had been saved. As Dick puts it so well, 'successes turned into failures, failures turned into successes'.

Overleaf:

Storyboards for *The Thief and the Cobbler*

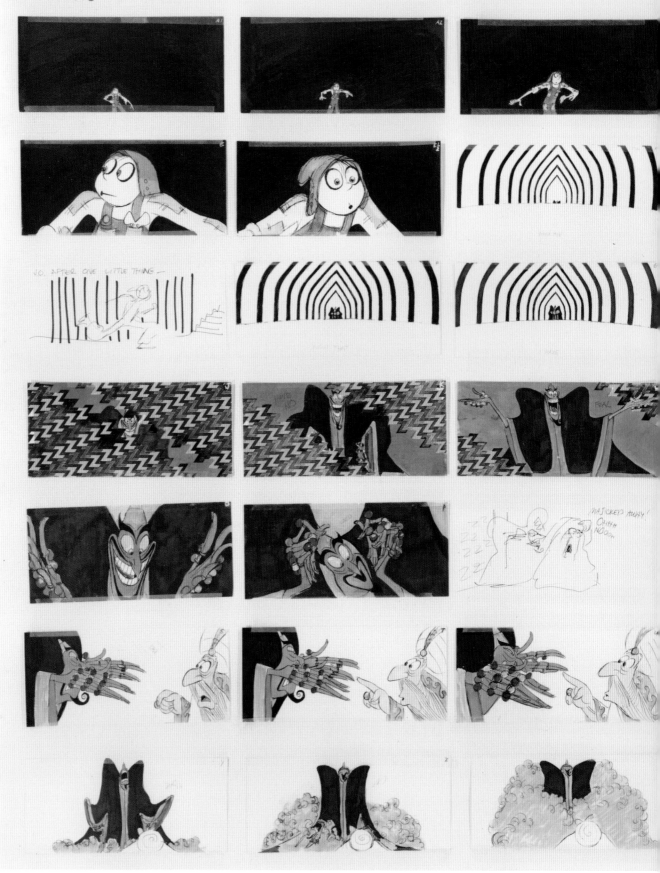

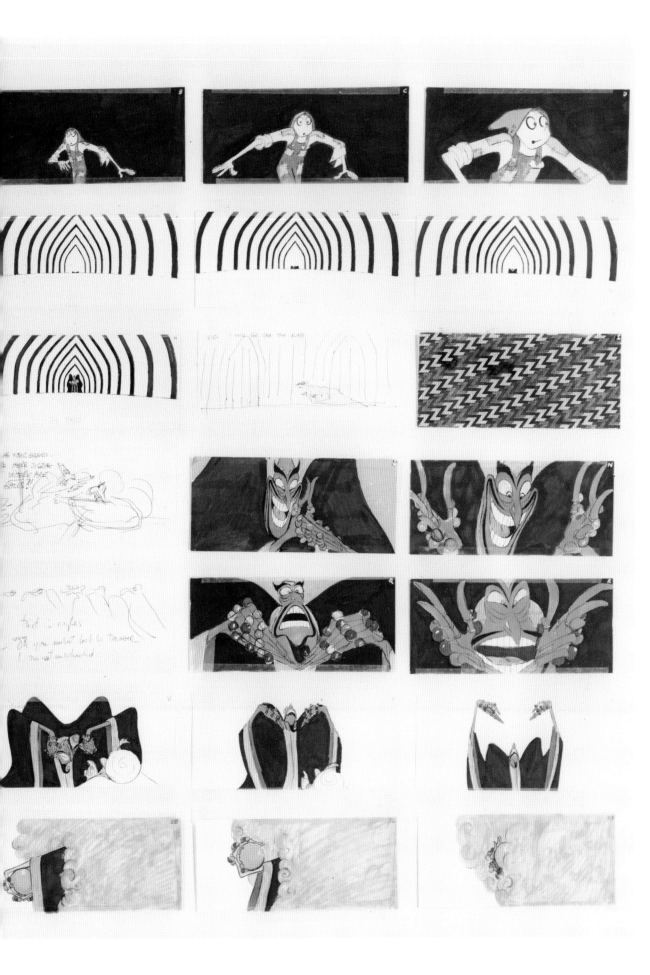

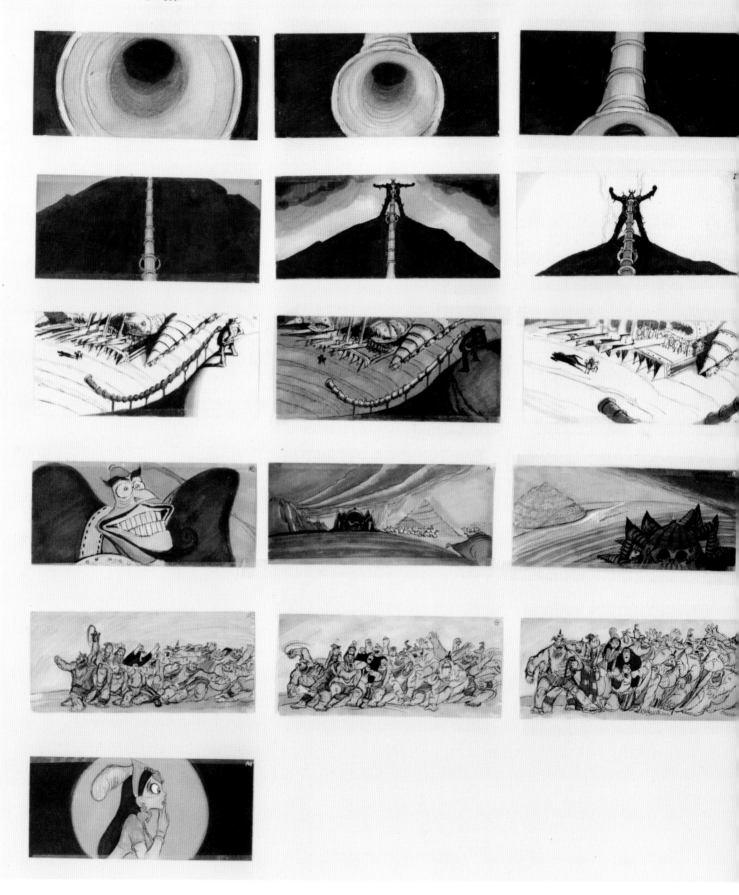

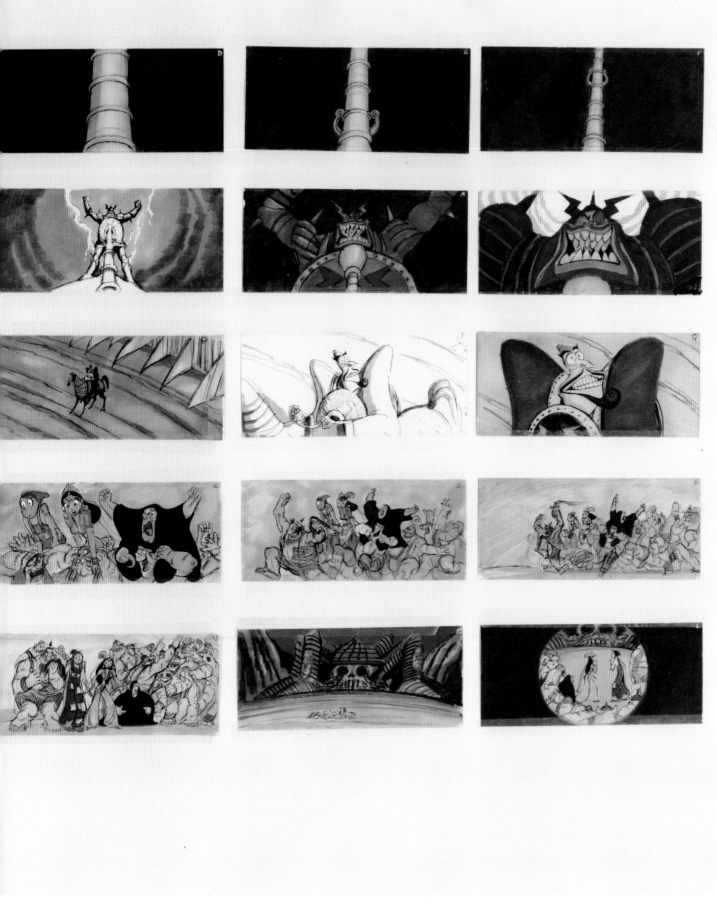

181

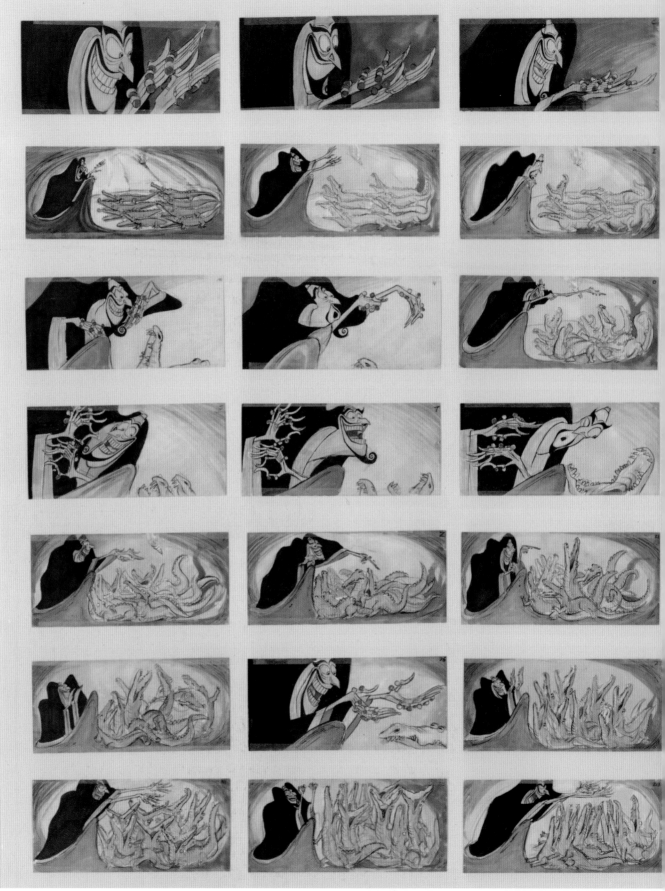

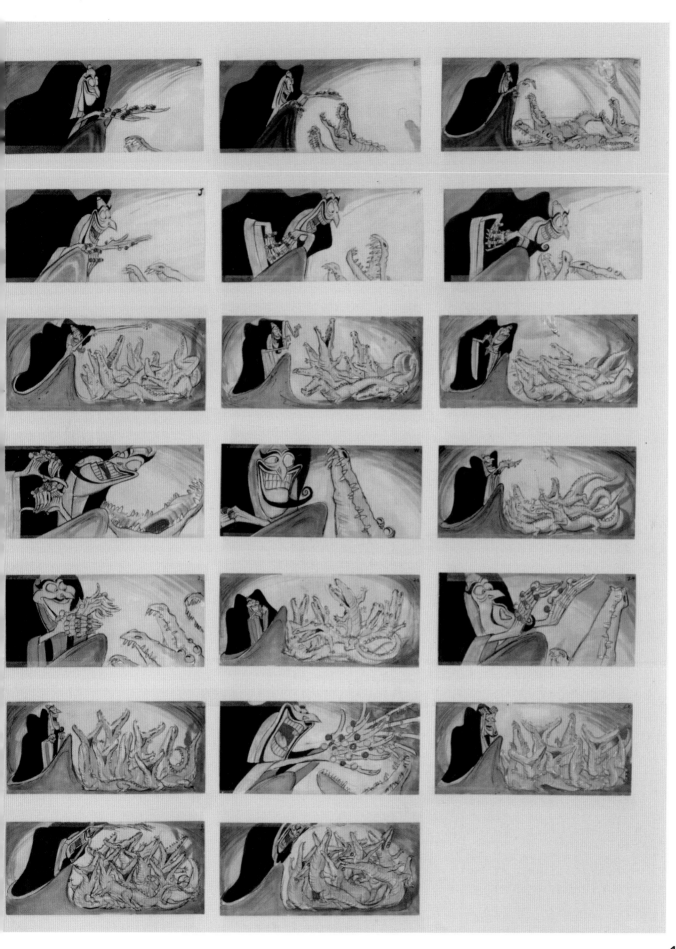

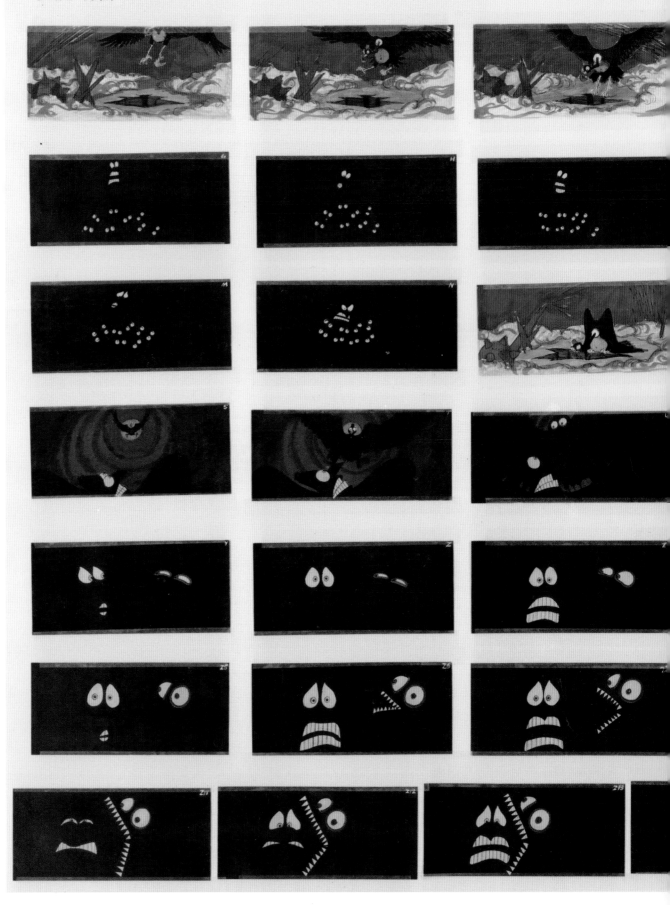

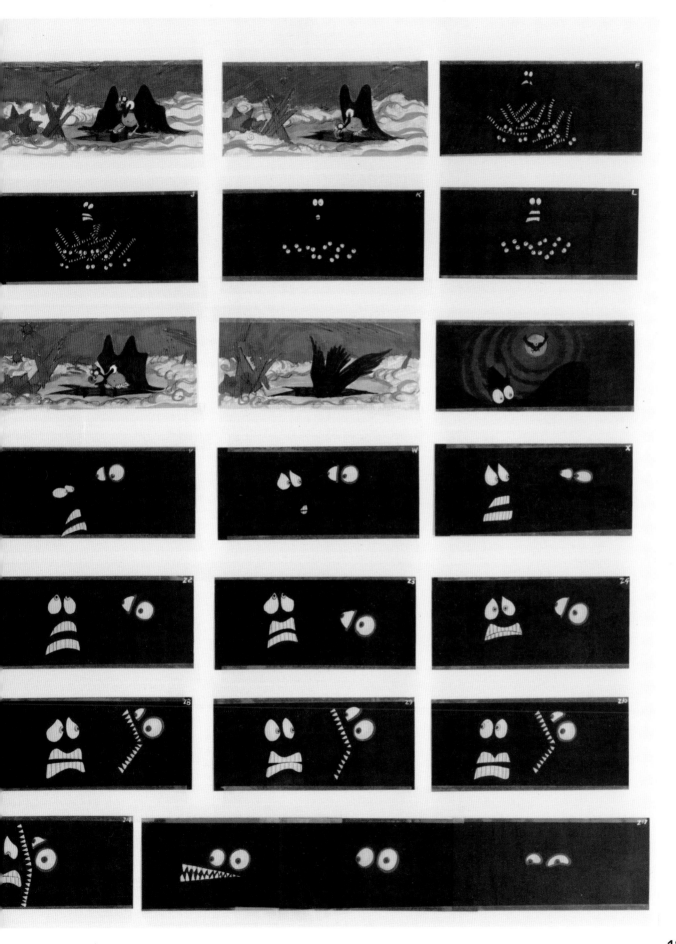

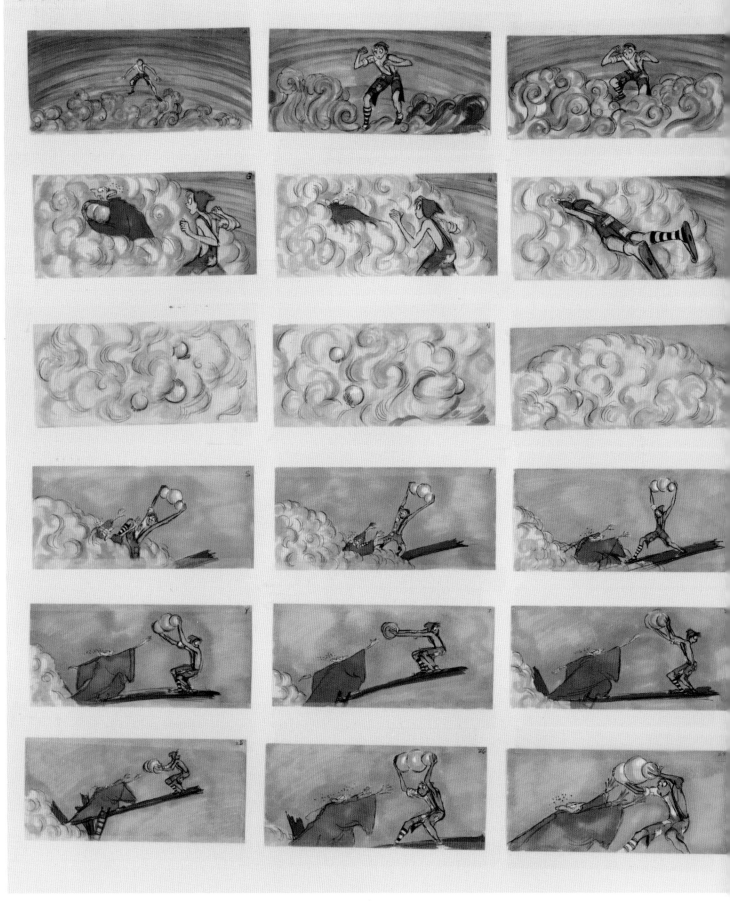

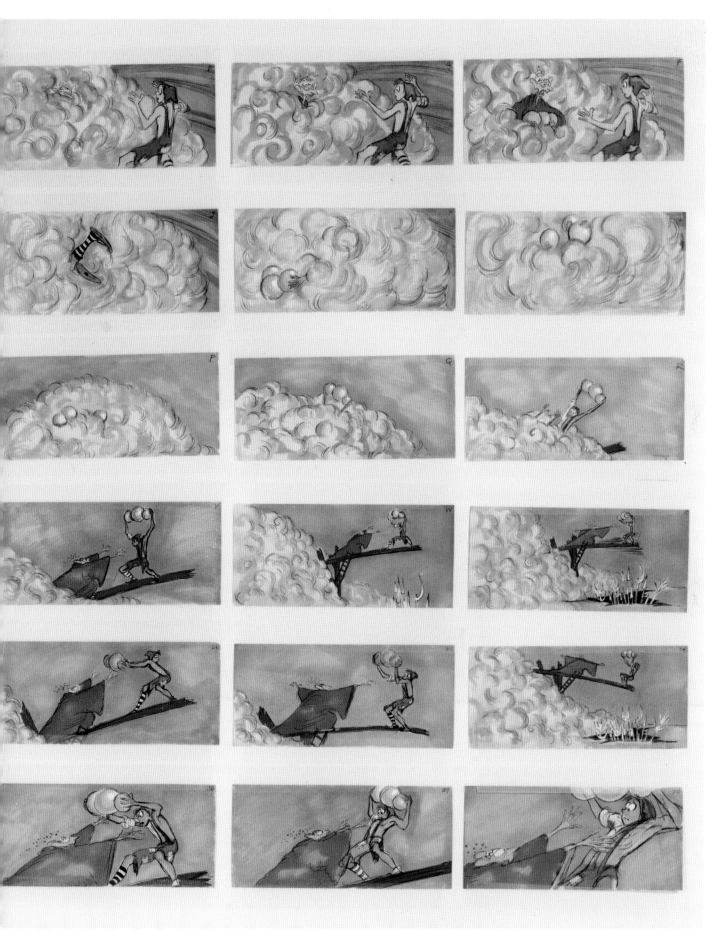

187

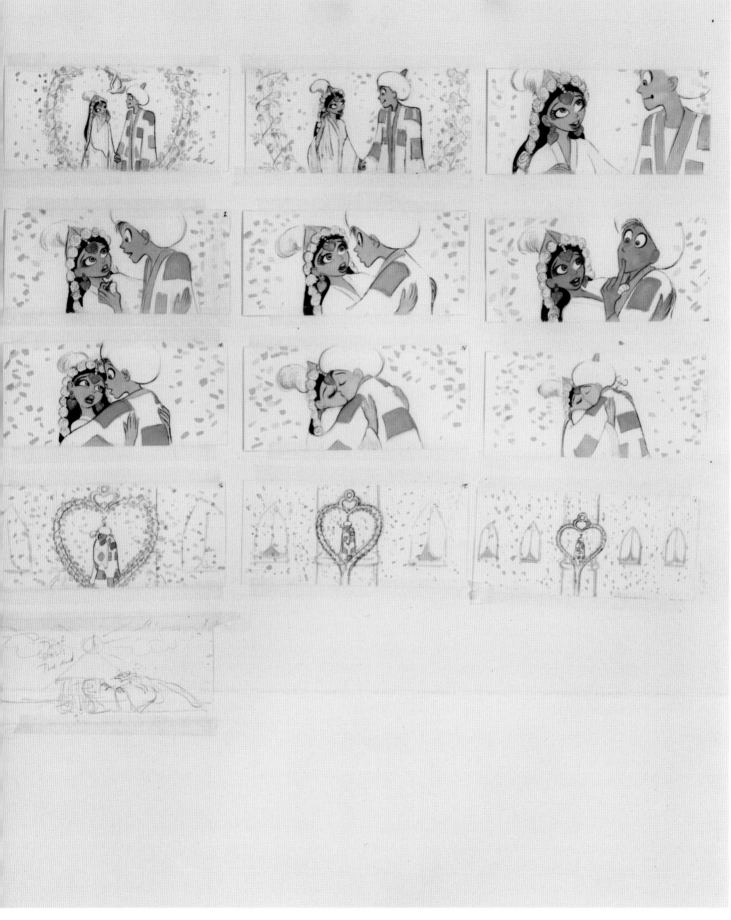

THE THIEF AND THE COBBLER: A MOMENT IN TIME

Since that screening in LA, the film has been screened in London, Annecy, New York, Montreal, Lille, Sitges and Barcelona.

At a screening in London at the BFI Southbank, Dick had this to say:

We did *The Thief and the Cobbler* on our own, paying for it with commercials – hundreds and hundreds of commercials for twenty years – then worked on it for another two years when the money came in. In fact, it's almost forty years in total because Ken Harris turned up forty years ago, halfway through my life, and *The Thief* kind of grew around Ken. Early on, I had another main character as well but that didn't work, so I lost it and started building the film around the Thief. Quite a lot of very good stuff had to go. Grim Natwick did a lot of crazy work on it; Emery Hawkins did some wonderful transitional morphing work, but we had to lose it all. The story was just too huge.

Grim Natwick did a funny walk on the Witch that set me going on her. My one regret is about the Witch. The main thing you can do with animation is morph it – the witch was going to turn into spaghetti. I had some really funny bits there, but that's as far as we got with the character.

The sound needed a lot of work, but there was just no time, we were slamming stuff in. But the voices were all great. Windsor Davies was the head of the brigands, Kenneth Williams and Stanley Baxter were the courtiers; they each did two voices. They were very good friends, although they were very competitive and had never worked together before, but I managed to get them to work together.

Anthony Quayle was the King. Vincent Price was Zigzag. It went on for about twenty years. Vincent was always willing to come in, as was Joan Sims as the Witch and the man who did the One-Eye voice – which sounds like it's a computerised voice, but it's not. I saw the tallest man in England on television and he had this very deep voice – imagine the voice box! We got in touch with him and asked: Would you do voices? – you've got this gigantic throat, you ought to be able to get deep sound. He hadn't tried it. So we worked with him and he discovered this tremendous deep voice.

Some of the music was done by David Cullen. He does Lloyd Webber's orchestrations. A couple of the other composers were musician friends of mine who I've played jazz with for years; they were completely new to it, but they did a fantastic job.

The credits were meant to go on the front of the film – a crystal ball was meant to come up slowly, and a pair of ancient, hundred-year-old hands would appear at the side of the crystal ball, and I was going to animate the hands, then put the credits on the sides.

The brigands were the only characters I didn't design. They were done by Corny Cole – and the brigands were based on his surfing friends. He designed all those guys. I had to draw them to fit in with the story. It was his work.

We had a fantastic crew. We had only four people in the administration: Mo, the producer, her secretary and two accountants. We ended up with a couple of hundred people and it ran like a top.

It's unfinished, but it's a thing of its own now. The Academy have it, it's in a golden box.

The Cobbler stitches the Thief

Princess Yumyum

Zigzag's trumpeters arrive in the city

Thief chased into a tree by polo ball

The Thief has finally reached the three golden balls

Zigzag's courtiers Goblet, Gopher, Slap and Tickle

King Nod pleads with boy to help his daughter

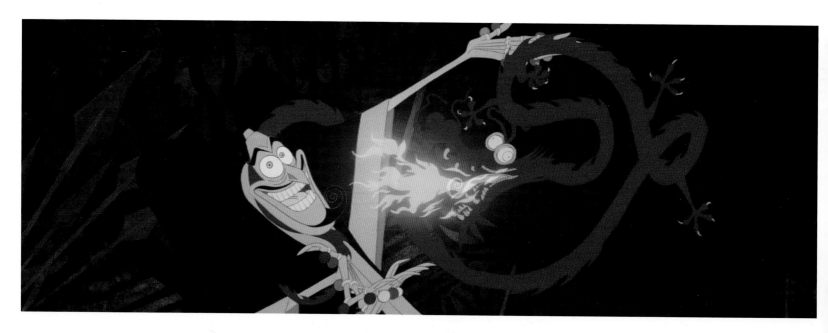

Zigzag's magic show for Mighty One-Eye

CIRCUS DRAWINGS:

THE FILM THAT TOOK FIFTY-SEVEN YEARS

Circus band: pencil drawing

After the DVDs were finished in 2010, we were drained. Rather than start something new, we decided to finish a film Dick had begun when he was a young man living on Ibiza. He'd finished *The Little Island* but *Circus Drawings* hadn't been completed. It was based on drawings he'd done of a Spanish circus. Dick describes what happened:

When I was in Ibiza, I lived in the Old City, and beyond the gate was a plain where, for two years, a Spanish circus would spend the winter. It was a very small gypsy circus, and even with my rotten Spanish, I became friendly with the acrobats – Peepy and his son Twon. I was fascinated by their movement. I liked the people a lot, and they put up with me drawing them. I thought it was a marvellous privilege.

At the time I didn't think about turning the drawings into a film. But back in London, I knew a good cameraman, and I said to him: I want to start shooting these drawings; I wanted him to zoom in on them. I wanted to make a short film where the camera appears to travel through the drawings. I wanted to get the quality of so-called fine art into animation, I thought my circus drawings had a sort of narrative to them: you see these people making up and getting ready for a performance. I intended to animate a short two-minute middle section and then the action would dry out and go back to drawings as the people took their make-up off, a sort of melancholy end.

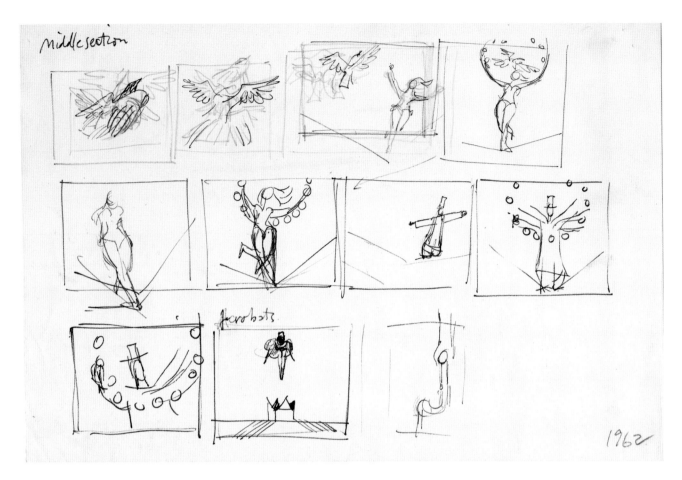

middle section

acrobats

1962

I was playing jazz all the time, and I showed the drawings to a couple of the guys in the band, and they mentioned Richard Rodney Bennett – a brilliant composer, but a jazzer as well. You should go see him, they said. So I did. I dumped my drawings on Richard's piano and said: I'd like an eight-piece, three-part movement, with these circus people – them preparing to perform, then a fast performance, and then just a quiet melancholic clean-up after.

And he said, 'Yeah, I'll do it,' and I said, 'Well, how much do you want?'

He said, 'You're not going to pay me, you'll pay the conductor, and you'll pay him well.'

Richard did an eight-piece score, recorded in 1965 – lovely, absolutely perfect. Though I had the soundtrack, I hadn't finished the picture, maybe 70 per cent of it had been filmed.

I carried it around all these different countries and then a few years ago I sat down and said, 'I'll finish this damn thing.' So I animated the middle section in colour. I'd take the original drawings, even if it was just a simple scribble of a dog or woman or whatever, and then move it, using my animation knowledge (about flexibility), and it came out fluid and snappy.

It's a wonderful film, partly because it shows the artist I was at 20 years old, and then the artist I was at 77. An eight-minute history of an artist.

197

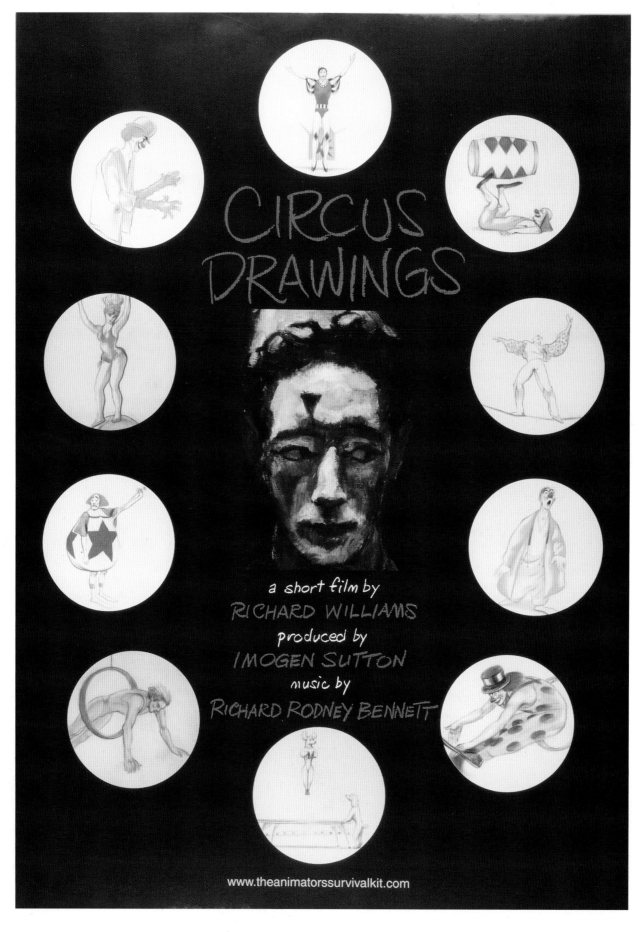

198

SILENT FILM LOGO

Dick again:

At about the same time as finishing *Circus Drawings* I made a silent film logo for the Giornate del Cinema Muto, a silent film festival in Pordenone. I'm a fanatic for great silent film stars. The main thing in animation is that it can do what no other form can do, which is to turn one thing into another. Like children draw in the corners of a page in a school book – they turn a flower into a sun, into a person, into a tree. We can do this morphing. I never really had a chance to turn one thing into another and I thought, I'm missing the main thing in animation. So as a present for the silent film festival and, in particular, for its director, my old friend David Robinson, I took Charlie Chaplin and turned him into Rudolph Valentino, turned Valentino into Greta Garbo and ended up at the other end with Buster Keaton and Laurel and Hardy.

What's interesting about animation is the middle position. Let's say you start with Valentino and he's going to turn into Garbo. So I've got two drawings and the one in the middle is going to be the interesting one where they're halfway. The drawings are clustered close together and then they turn into the middle position and they cluster at the end where they slow up.

I animated this logo with no soundtrack so that the silent film accompanists could either play the piano or in a group.

Moving through Stan and Ollie

PROLOGUE

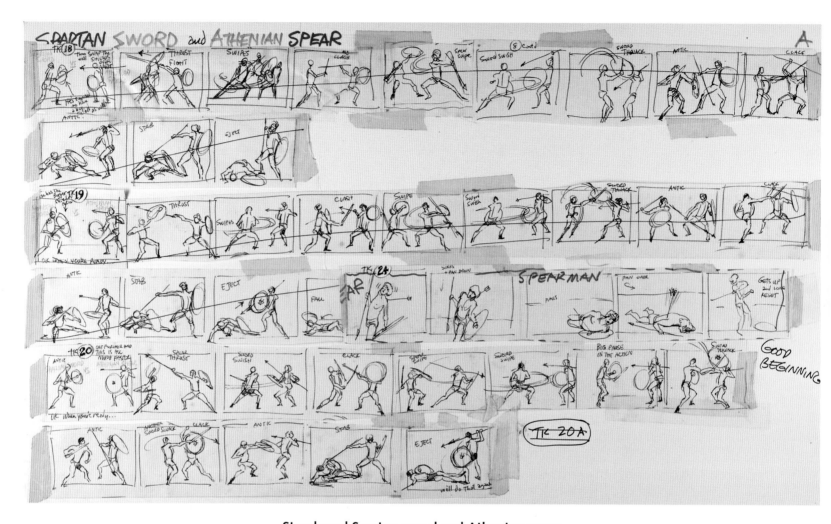

Storyboard Spartan sword and Athenian spear

Dick had read Aristophanes' *Lysistrata* as a teenager in an edition illustrated with erotic drawings by the Australian artist Norman Lindsay. The story of *Lysistrata* is of women who go on a sex strike to stop their menfolk fighting in a war between Athens and Sparta. It's a story that has been adapted in many ways and Dick had always wanted to animate it, but it was only in his late 70s that he felt up to the task.

Before we left London for Canada, we had seen a pub version of *Lysistrata* – which opened with four young men miming a fight between the Spartans and the Athenians. Dick thought a battle scene would make a good prologue to a film version and asked the actors if he could do life drawings of their actions as a way of understanding the movements of a man with a spear, an axe, a sword or a bow. He took these drawings to Salt Spring and did more life drawings that he could use as a basis for animation.

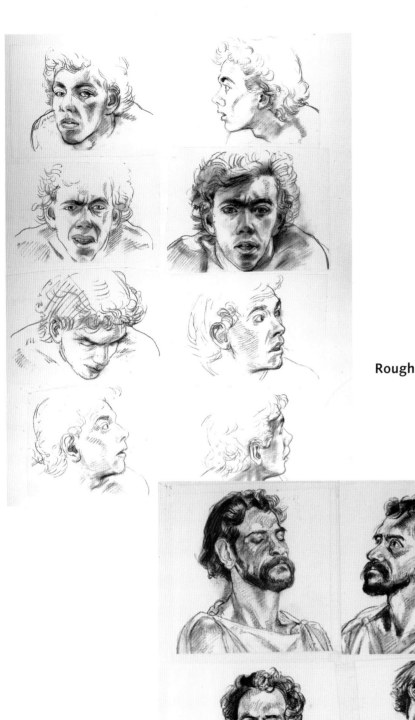

Rough drafts of Athenian axeman

Rough drafts of Spartan archer

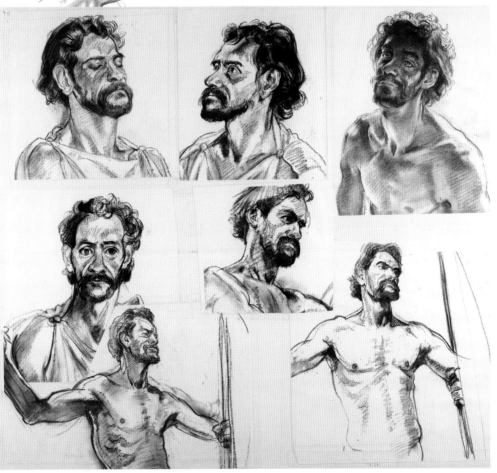

201

When we moved to Wales, he began work on it. He planned to animate the film alone, using only pencil and paper. The film was to be one continuous shot – he would draw the camera moves. This was to be the culmination of a lifetime of work and study.

My concern was how long it would take to finish such an ambitious project. So one day when we were sitting in a café in Pordenone, where we were enjoying the stimulating experience of watching great silent movies at the Giornate del Cinema Muto, I made a suggestion: why didn't we make the film in chapters? We'd take one section of the film at a time, finish it, and then move onto the next. This would give Dick the satisfaction of completing one short film and then starting another.

So the prologue to the film *Lysistrata* became *Prologue*, a six-minute film. Dick started the film with a short, live action sequence where you see the hundreds of pencil stubs he'd produced over the making of the film; you then see him place a still drawing of a foxglove on his drawing board, which dissolves into animation of a bee entering the flower. The rest of the film is a battle to the death between two Athenians and two Spartans with a coda to link it to the next film – a young girl is horrified by what she sees and runs to tell her grandmother.

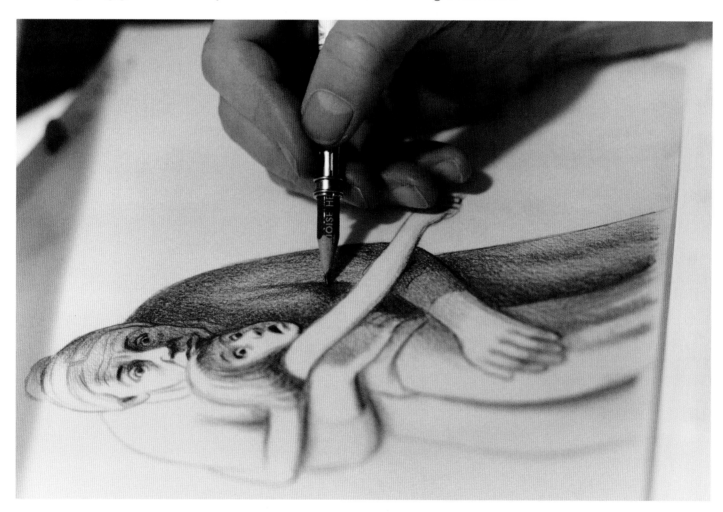

Drawing the old woman and girl

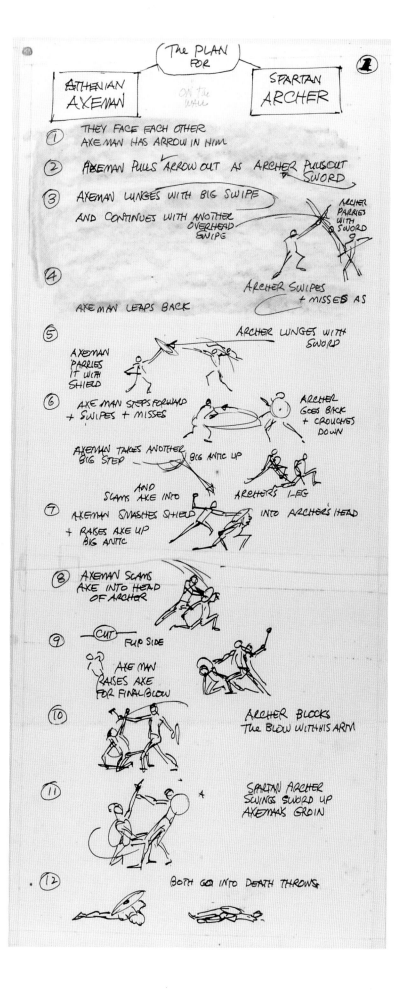

The PLAN FOR

ON the WALL

ATHENIAN AXEMAN

SPARTAN ARCHER

1 THEY FACE EACH OTHER
AXEMAN HAS ARROW IN HIM

2 AXEMAN PULLS ARROW OUT AS ARCHER PULLS OUT SWORD

3 AXEMAN LUNGES WITH BIG SWIPE

AND CONTINUES WITH ANOTHER OVERHEAD SWIPE

ARCHER PARRIES WITH SWORD

4 ARCHER SWIPES + MISSES AS

AXEMAN LEAPS BACK

5 ARCHER LUNGES WITH SWORD

AXEMAN PARRIES IT WITH SHIELD

6 AXEMAN STEPS FORWARD + SWIPES + MISSES

ARCHER GOES BACK + CROUCHES DOWN

AXEMAN TAKES ANOTHER BIG STEP — BIG ANTIC UP

AND SLAMS AXE INTO ARCHER'S LEG

7 AXEMAN SMASHES SHIELD INTO ARCHER'S HEAD

+ RAISES AXE UP BIG ANTIC

8 AXEMAN SLAMS AXE INTO HEAD OF ARCHER

9 CUT FLIP SIDE

OR AXE MAN RAISES AXE FOR FINAL BLOW

10 ARCHER BLOCKS THE BLOW WITH HIS ARM

11 SPARTAN ARCHER SWINGS SWORD UP AXEMAN'S GROIN

12 BOTH GO INTO DEATH THROWS

203

This is what Dick had to say about it:

I had an idea for a big film when I was 15 years old and I wondered if I would ever get good enough to do this. It's something that nobody had done before. About eight years ago something happened to me. I don't know – with all this teaching, all this experience – it's like yogurt, it finally just took, and I'm able to do exactly what I can imagine.

People say, 'What's this film about?'

I say, 'Well, I'll tell you the working title – *Will I Live to Finish This?*'

I really hope I can stretch this out because it's an enormous amount of work and I'm into territory where people have tried to go before and haven't brought it off.

I keep thinking, animation is so much work and you have to learn. That's why I was reluctant after my first film – you have to learn so much. I don't want to do stuff that just looks like cartoons, but to make drawings that walk and talk. You can put them anywhere, you can do anything. It just seemed that it would be such a hard journey of learning how to do all this stuff. 'Cos I wanted the whole ball of wax.

A lot of animators can be very funny, but they do one kind of thing. I wanted the whole whammy. I'm artistically greedy, or at least artistically ambitious. That was my goal. I thought it doesn't matter what I do – I've got to master this damn thing so I can do anything I want. Fortunately, I've achieved it when I'm still reasonably healthy and walking around.

With Mo at the 2015 screening of *Prologue* at the Annecy International Animation Festival

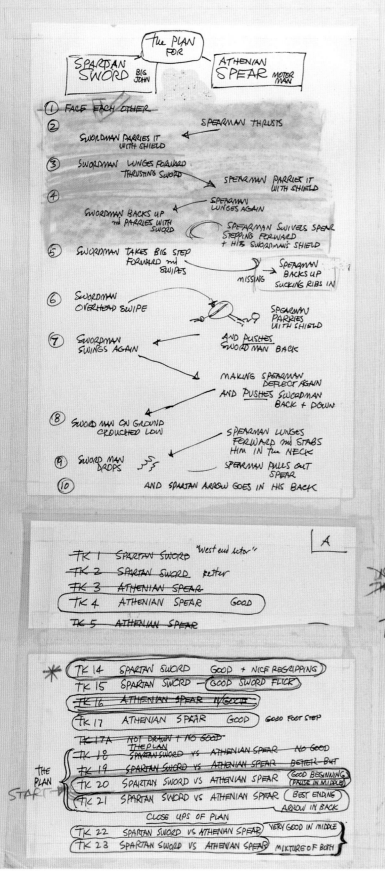

The PLAN FOR

SPARTAN SWORD (BIG JOHN) | ATHENIAN SPEAR (MOTOR MAN)

1. FACE EACH OTHER
2. SPEARMAN THRUSTS / SWORDMAN PARRIES IT WITH SHIELD
3. SWORDMAN LUNGES FORWARD THRUSTING SWORD / SPEARMAN PARRIES IT WITH SHIELD
4. SWORDMAN BACKS UP AND PARRIES WITH SWORD / SPEARMAN LUNGES AGAIN / SPEARMAN SWIVELS SPEAR STEPPING FORWARD + HITS SWORDMAN'S SHIELD
5. SWORDMAN TAKES BIG STEP FORWARD AND SWIPES — MISSING → SPEARMAN BACKS UP SUCKING RIBS IN
6. SWORDMAN OVERHEAD SWIPE / SPEARMAN PARRIES WITH SHIELD
7. SWORDMAN SWINGS AGAIN / AND PUSHES SWORDMAN BACK / MAKING SPEARMAN DEFLECT AGAIN / AND PUSHES SWORDMAN BACK + DOWN
8. SWORDMAN ON GROUND CROUCHED LOW / SPEARMAN LUNGES FORWARD AND STABS HIM IN THE NECK
9. SWORDMAN DROPS / SPEARMAN PULLS OUT SPEAR
10. AND SPARTAN ARROW GOES IN HIS BACK

A

TK 1   SPARTAN SWORD   "West end actor"
TK 2   SPARTAN SWORD   better
TK 3   ATHENIAN SPEAR
TK 4   ATHENIAN SPEAR   GOOD
TK 5   ATHENIAN SPEAR

★ TK 14   SPARTAN SWORD   GOOD + NICE REGRIPPING
TK 15   SPARTAN SWORD — GOOD SWORD FLICK
TK 16   ATHENIAN SPEAR   N/GOOD
TK 17   ATHENIAN SPEAR   GOOD   GOOD FOOT STEP
TK 17A   NOT DRAWN + NO GOOD
THE PLAN
TK 18   SPARTAN SWORD VS ATHENIAN SPEAR   NO GOOD
TK 19   SPARTAN SWORD VS ATHENIAN SPEAR   BETTER BUT
TK 20   SPARTAN SWORD VS ATHENIAN SPEAR   GOOD BEGINNING (PAUSE IN MIDDLE)
THE PLAN
TK 21   SPARTAN SWORD VS ATHENIAN SPEAR   BEST ENDING — ARROW IN BACK
START →
CLOSE UPS OF PLAN
TK 22   SPARTAN SWORD VS ATHENIAN SPEAR   VERY GOOD IN MIDDLE
TK 23   SPARTAN SWORD VS ATHENIAN SPEAR   MIXTURE OF BOTH

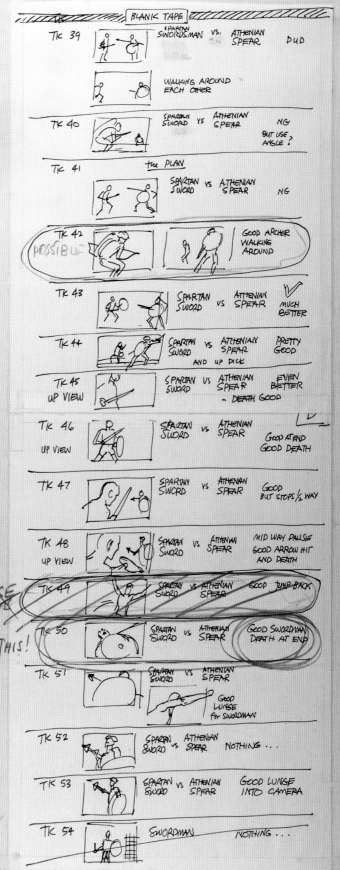

BLANK TAPE

TK 39   SPARTAN SWORDSMAN VS. ATHENIAN SPEAR   DUD
WALKING AROUND EACH OTHER
TK 40   SPARTAN SWORD VS ATHENIAN SPEAR   NG BUT USE ANGLE?
TK 41   THE PLAN   SPARTAN SWORD VS ATHENIAN SPEAR   NG
TK 42   POSSIBLE   GOOD ARCHER WALKING AROUND
TK 43   SPARTAN SWORD VS ATHENIAN SPEAR   MUCH BETTER ✓
TK 44   SPARTAN SWORD VS ATHENIAN SPEAR   AND UP DICK   PRETTY GOOD
TK 45   UP VIEW   SPARTAN SWORD VS ATHENIAN SPEAR   EVEN BETTER - DEATH GOOD
TK 46   UP VIEW   SPARTAN SWORD VS ATHENIAN SPEAR   GOOD AT END GOOD DEATH
TK 47   SPARTAN SWORD VS ATHENIAN SPEAR   GOOD BUT STOPS ½ WAY
TK 48   UP VIEW   SPARTAN SWORD VS ATHENIAN SPEAR   MID WAY PAUSE GOOD ARROW HIT AND DEATH
TK 49   SPARTAN SWORD VS ATHENIAN SPEAR   GOOD JUMP BACK
USE THIS   TK 50   SPARTAN SWORD VS ATHENIAN SPEAR   GOOD SWORDMAN DEATH AT END
THIS!
TK 51   SPARTAN SWORD VS ATHENIAN SPEAR   GOOD LUNGE FOR SWORDMAN
TK 52   SPARTAN SWORD VS ATHENIAN SPEAR   NOTHING...
TK 53   SPARTAN SWORD VS ATHENIAN SPEAR   GOOD LUNGE INTO CAMERA
TK 54   SWORDMAN   NOTHING...

Directed by **Richard Williams**

PROLOGUE

Produced by **Imogen Sutton**

In 2015, we screened the film at a few film festivals and then in a Los Angeles theatre, which made it eligible for the Oscar selection process. We were so nervous the day the nominations were to be announced that we just lay on our bed unable to move. I'd miscalculated the time difference between LA and Bristol and we thought we had another hour to wait when my phone started buzzing. A friend had heard our names on the BBC news. We guessed that meant we were nominated.

Dick started work immediately on the next chapter of the film, *A Call to Arms*. It would introduce the main women characters and their plan to go on a sex strike to stop the war. *Prologue* had no dialogue. In *A Call to Arms* there was to be a mix of serious political activism and comic, bawdy dialogue. Dick had often recorded voices for films – he was Droopy in *Who Framed Roger Rabbit* – and I had done narration for documentaries. I played the serious role of Lysistrata, Dick played the comic character Neeki. Every now and then we'd go to a studio to record some of the script. Sometimes our daughter, Natasha, who is an actor, came too. She played the seductive Myrrhina.

Neeki

Aardman were once again providing us with facilities – Tom Barnes and Tony Prescott arranged a large room, an animation desk and a camera. As each scene was finished, Fernando Lechuga would do the compositing. The film was being built scene by scene, and at every viewing I couldn't wait to see more.

By the time Dick became ill in 2019, he had completed about six minutes of what was to be a ten-minute film. He didn't live to finish it.

TWEETS @RWANIMATOR

Anatomy – 29/07/2015
I restudy anatomy when I'm travelling or on holiday. Otherwise I'm animating my own stuff full time.

Mistakes – 04/10/2015
Value mistakes. I still goof at 82.

Milt – 24/12/2016
I'm studying the master Milt Kahl. His work is perfect. What an intelligence. I always discover new things in his scenes.

Prologue – 12/02/2016
Dick says, 'Wow! Our film PROLOGUE has been nominated for an Oscar. Mo and I thrilled.'
'It's the first film I've done that I've been happy with.'

The book – 09/08/2017
I have to use it myself sometimes. Was in a bookshop yesterday and picked it up. There's certainly a hell of a lot of stuff in it.

Ken Harris – 08/10/2017
I watched Ken Harris's animation of Bugs Bunny frame by frame as a kid.

Lucky – 08/10/2017
I was unusually lucky to have known and worked with the best. I wanted this knowledge to live.

March time and general timing – 22/10/2017
Ways to time things. Milt Kahl used march time – every twelve frames. So everything is either slightly more than march time or slightly less than march time. That worked for him.
Something I still find very useful for timing long scenes is an old-fashioned music metronome. I act things out to the desired beat.

Inspiration – 28/10/2017
We all need inspiration and I get it from so many sources, artists and filmmakers – Akira Kurosawa, Milt Kahl, Heinrich Kley et al.

Pleased not proud – 28/10/2017

I'm never proud but recently pleased with *The Thief*, *Prologue*, *The Animator's Survival Kit* book, iPad app.

The animated logo of *The Animator's Survival Kit* – 28/10/2017

The logo took Neil Boyle and me nine months to animate. Mark Naisbitt same to paint. Pieter Van Houte shot it.

Responding to a student who wants to expand their knowledge – 28/10/2017

Read my book or get the iPad app and see everything you can – films, paintings, books, plays. Devour everything.

Blinking – 29/10/2017

It's all to do with who the character is. Nervous people blink all the time. Secure people blink less. Watch people on TV.

On in-betweens – 29/10/2017

Don't do finished in-betweens until you have the animation sorted. Pose to pose the straight ahead runs on parts. Important parts first.

Timing and acting it out – 29/10/2017

Act it out till it feels right or have someone else act it out to your timing.

Milt – 19/11/2017 and 31/10/2017

I'm increasingly conscious of arcs when working. The master of arcs is Milt Kahl. Study Milt Kahl. You can always learn by copying. Work rough so you can alter.

On ones and twos and *Roger Rabbit* – 19/11/2017

When the camera is moving you must use ones. When the camera is locked off you can get away with twos unless of course the animation is moving in relation to a moving character, then you've obviously got to be on ones. An example – Jessica and Roger on the hook were all on twos.

In normal animation we use ones and twos. It's not just twos or just ones – which some people think. It's like saying do you use red or blue? You use both. Ones for fast action and twos for general action. Also use ones when an action goes across the screen, otherwise it strobes.

On *The Animator's Survival Kit* – 19/11/2017

The Animator's Survival Kit has got an awful lot of stuff in it. It took me a lifetime to learn and four years to pack it in as simply as possible.

I always thought someone's got to do it and was surprised it turned out to be me. It sometimes gets me out of a jam too. It was always meant to be a working tool.

On Droopy [RW did the voice in *Who Framed Roger Rabbit*] – 01/12/2017
I've always loved Droopy and Tex Avery.

On animating Neeki in *A Call to Arms* – 05/12/2017
I have a new character and I really love animating her. She tells me what to do.

On 13 Soho Square – 07/12/2017
When I pass the building I think of Ken Harris, Art Babbitt, Grim Natwick and a marvellous artist I worked with – Errol Le Cain – working with me and Roy Naisbitt. It was a unique time in a great place.

On Twitter following reaching 10,000 – 06/12/2017
I'm astonished to learn today there are more than 10,000 followers for @RWAnimator. This has gone to my head which is now so large I can't get it through the door to my studio. Thank you everybody. I'm honoured.

On the award – 07/12/2017
Tomorrow I'm very honoured to be the recipient of the first Lotte Reiniger Lifetime Achievement Award. I spent an evening with Lotte Reiniger when I was 23 years old. She was a really interesting artist, famed for her silhouette animation. A real pioneer.

On meeting students at the European Animation Awards where he received a Lifetime Achievement award – 08/12/2017
I don't see you all as students but as young artists. I was a young artist once and now I'm an old one. That's what we are.

NAPKIN MESSAGE – 21/12/2017
'Thanks to all our followers. Merry Christmas.'

Believability – 10/01/2018
Getting weight seems to be the hardest thing for animators to achieve. Especially when they rotoscope or semi-rotoscope things. I'm glad to see such interest in this aspect of getting believability.

Real craft – 11/01/2018
What I love about animation is that it is a real craft – you can't fake it.

Artist and garage mechanic – 11/01/2018

Preston Blair said, 'An animator is something between an artist and a garage mechanic.'
I agree. But the garage mechanic bit takes a while. So does the artist part.

The book 'ain't just for beginners' – 14/01/2018

The Animator's Survival Kit ain't just for beginners – the idea was to cover the whole spectrum of knowledge developed since 1925. I consult the book myself sometimes to get the desired result.

Slipping back into old working habits – 18/01/2018

Interesting thing this week. I got into trouble when I slipped back into working the way I used to before I learned from the old guys. I wasn't doing the garage mechanic part. I thought I'd better read my own book. Turned my head around and sorted the mess out in a twinkling.

On working hard and doing the best work at 84 – 18/01/2018

I'm working hard and doing my best work. I am enjoying it more than ever.

Concentration – 04/02/2018

There's no substitution for concentration. I find it's always better to concentrate without music. Mistakes are made when we're too relaxed.

Milt – 05/02/2018

Milt was mercurial, didn't suffer fools gladly but was enormously generous and kind.

Clarity – 11/02/2018

The older I get the more I realise how important it is to have a very clear idea of what you want to achieve – well before you animate. If your idea is really clear there is still room to improvise as you go along, but make sure at the start you really picture your exact goal.

Starting a studio – 11/02/2018

My answer is to start small based on your own work and go for quality not quantity.

Animating all day – 12/02/2018

Dick is asked in a tweet how much time out of the day he animates. He replies: 'All day.'

Learning from mistakes – 12/02/2018

I've got things wrong all through my life and it's true we learn from our mistakes not our successes. For me it's challenging not frustrating.

We all have difficulties. It ain't easy. Milt Kahl was having real trouble with a complex cycle and Marc Davis said, 'If you really WERE God things would come out first time.'

Inspiration – 16/02/2018

There have been some questions about where I find inspiration – I have always been inspired by and learned from silent films. Comic and serious. Especially Charlie Chaplin, Buster Keaton and Laurel and Hardy. I can't help studying their movement, timing and invention.

Add Fred Astaire, Cyd Charisse and Ann Miller to that list. Great dancers with those extra moves. My favourite director/writer/editor is Akira Kurosawa – ever since *Rashomon* I've loved all his films. Stunning.

Persistence – 01/03/2018

Just keep at it. It's hard so you have to persist. Hand and brain co-ordination.

Walks – 01/03/2018 and 03/03/2018

When people ask my advice on 'how can I improve or make things better?' there is a real answer. Do walks. Walks of all kinds. If you can do walks convincingly you can do anything. It takes persistence. Copy and invent your own. My book has over eighty pages on walks.

About doing walks: to avoid wearing yourself out, work with very simple drawings. To get the benefit don't do complicated drawings. Put the complications or inventions in the movement with simple lines.

Strengths – 03/03/2018

Go with your strengths. Go with what is most natural to you.

Clay – 10/03/2018

I think animation is like clay – keep pushing it around if you have the time.

On copying and being unoriginal – 10/03/2018

On the subject of copying and being unoriginal – we learn by copying and we unconsciously steal. Michael Caine said in his Masterclass – if you see a bit of acting business you like then STEAL IT. Because THEY DID.

On walks and character – 10/03/2018

I'm not thinking about animation and then I see one of these crazy walks. So I immediately analyse it. Some of these walks are unbelievable. Walks are character for all to see. Top actors say getting the character's walk is the first thing they do.

Heinrich Kley – 18/03/2018

I've always been an admirer of Heinrich Kley, a great German artist of the 1910s and 1920s.
Kley is really worth studying as is the work of his friend Käthe Kollwitz. Both inspiring

antidotes to bad drawing. In the 1930s Walt Disney travelled to Europe and discovered Kley. He bought as many of his drawings as he could and took them to his top artists.

Disney said to his artists, 'Why can't you guys draw like that?' Nobody could but they used Kley's work as inspiration for the alligators, elephants and hippos in *Fantasia*. When the great Ken Harris died he left me a large book of Kley's work. He's astonishing.

Cheating things – 25/03/2018
Cheating things sometimes works. If it works, it works. But of course you feel better when you've done it the way it ought to be.

Lip sync – 25/03/2018
Lip sync in phrases. You phrase from one mouth shape to another.

Dick talking about *Roger Rabbit* – 26/03/2018
That's the rule of animation: you have to do what you can't do with a camera . . . so every element in animation should have an element of impossibility.

On paper and pencil – 31/03/2018
I'm on paper and pencil. Someone asked, 'What is that software you're using?' I said, 'It's called 3B.'

Mirrors – 31/03/2018
Art Babbitt said that we don't need mirrors – we've advanced past that point. But I find that they are very useful for timing, dialogue and, for example, the amount of stretch in a face. Also how fast a hand gesture is. Lots of uses.

More on mirrors – 31/03/2018
I'm having a moment of not knowing quite how a character should behave. So back to my own advice: act it out until it feels right and in front of a mirror. Then analyse it. Sleep on it. Then do it.

Maintaining the forms – 01/04/2018
I'm afraid it's a lot of work and it's always work to maintain the forms. It ain't easy.

On a scene with a moving camera – 01/04/2018
I'd approach it the same way I would do a normal scene. Do the contacts first. If you don't have contacts then block in the main positions like fence posts – taking into account perspective. Then break it down with passing positions. Then keep breaking it down into bits.

Milt and the double bounce – 02/04/2018

I asked Milt how he did an amazing double bounce walk in *Medusa*. I asked if he used a model. He said, 'Nope, I closed the door, acted it out and hoped nobody came in.'

On motivation – 02/04/2018

I think the answer is to just start. Never mind how you feel. It all changes when you start.

Live action – 03/04/2018

You use bits – suggestions that you might never think of. It's information and it depends how you use it.

Importance of anatomy – 06/04/2018

Athletes know how the muscles work. We should have some idea of it in order to get convincing movement and weight into the work. Knowledge doesn't hurt – it helps.

Rotoscoping – 06/04/2018

Rotoscoping keeps coming up. Whatever turns you on but for more detail my *Animator's Survival Kit* book goes into the nitty gritty.

For me live action is just a source of information. Milt learned so much from studying it that in the end he refused to look at it – he knew it.

On storyboarding – 08/04/2018

Look at Kurosawa's films. He storyboarded the whole of *Kagemusha* in colour. Study silent films. The language of clarity.

Swimming – 10/04/2018

I swim half a mile every morning except on weekends.

Sound design – 10/04/2018

Sound design is an art form all of its own. But give it your best shot until it sounds right to you.

The unknown factor – 15/04/2018

Every now and then when I'm working on something I ask someone to do some poses for me. More often than not they'll come up with something more interesting than I would have thought of – that fits the bill. It's the unknown factor that gets you off more usual patterns.

Life drawing – 15/04/2018

Life drawing is the best teacher. Draw all the time. Study the great artists. I'm off to the National Gallery in London today – I keep studying.

Music and animation – 24/04/2018

I think of everything rhythmically and I love tight sync and hitting the accents. I'm a semi-pro musician so it's natural. I love the lost art of early 'Mickey Mousing' but I wouldn't want it for everything.

Too much action – 25/04/2018

A mistake many of us make is to put too much action in too short a space of time. The remedy is to be clear about what you're going to do, and time it in your head – or with a stopwatch – well before you do it. It's a problem I'm always aware of when I'm working.

On making a short film – 05/05/2018

Have a strong idea and be clear.

On imagination – 05/05/2018

I think we have to take the normal imagination we've got and concentrate on our executive ability to put the ideas over. That's where the work and invention lie.

Timing and using a metronome – 05/05/2018

Here's my old metronome still working. Here's the other side of the metronome with the animation frames marked on the left with the metronome speeds on the right. So if I'm acting out a twelve-frame walk I turn on the metronome at 120 and walk around to that timing. I'm sure there are more modern ways of doing this.

On *Prologue* as one shot – 03/06/2018

In *Prologue* it's all in one shot and I don't move the camera – I just draw all the moves. In order to do this I use my knowledge of movement. It's all in the timing and the spacing – just like in character animation.

On continuous learning – 18/06/2018

I'm always learning and I'm always finding new stuff when I'm working. And I go back and study the work that has impressed me. Milt is always fascinating.

Commenting on a piece of animation – 27/06/2018

Too much action in too short a space of time. Drawing is learning to draw by drawing all the time. Life drawing teaches everything.

Subtle stuff – 27/06/2018

Subtle stuff is hard to do if you don't understand the basics properly. If you know the basics you will be able to select the key positions and ease in and out effectively. Practise the basics.

Copy in order to understand. It's all in the book.

Silent movies – 29/07/2018
Study silent movies. Great idea. I've done it all my life.

Working with multiple characters – 29/07/2018
Something on working with multiple characters: start with the most important one in the centre then build the next one in relation to the first one. Then add in the next important one in relation to the first two and so on. I have just done this with two groups of women . . . all heads and shoulders. In this case I drew everything on one sheet of paper and exposed on twos. But the timing charts and the spacing I did individually so that it's different for each character – in spite of the whole thing being on twos. It works and was enjoyable to do.

Advice for young animators – 01/08/2018
Tell them if they enjoy drawing to draw. And if they work with plasticine and like it – just do lots and lots of it. Do lots of what you love. Whatever it is.

Timing and contemporary animation – 04/08/2018
I've just seen a film where the slow bits are too slow and the fast bits too fast. Timing is the thing which dominates everything. Doesn't matter if Leonardo da Vinci does the drawings – timing is the most important thing to get right.

On timing and *The Little Island* – 04/08/2018
I got a rave review for my first film *The Little Island*, but the critic also said, 'Williams doesn't yet know enough about timing.' Right on. The timing dominates – look at Chaplin, Keaton, Laurel and Hardy, Chuck Jones, Tex Avery.

Works to study for timing – 04/08/2018
Try *One Froggy Evening* – a Chuck Jones short – or Tex Avery's *King-Size Canary*. In *Dumbo* – the pink elephants sequence. Any Charlie Chaplin or Buster Keaton.

Posing versus timing – 04/08/2018
Obviously posing and everything else has to be right. I'm just saying these are motion pictures and the timing of the motion dominates.

What should I do if I want to be an animator when I'm older? – 29/08/2018
First, draw your ass off. Second, study Milt. Good luck with it.

How do you get back on track? – 12/09/2018

I put bum on seat and start. There's a great Japanese saying. 'Starting is half'.

Re life drawing if no classes – 12/09/2018

Use whatever you can. I often cut a photograph out of the paper that I can use. Anything I can get my hands on. There are lots of life drawing classes around these days – hope you can find one. Always good if you can have the real thing but use whatever you can.

On someone owning two copies of the *The Animator's Survival Kit* – one for home and one for work – 26/10/2018

I also have one for home and one for work.

Someone having problems bringing things 'to life' – 26/10/2018

All I can say is carry on, keep going and it will come to life.

Someone reading the book who has to start all over again – 26/10/2018

I had the same reaction when I met the great animators like Ken Harris and Milt Kahl. I had to start again.

Learning vibrations – 26/10/2018

There are so many vibration formulas in the book. I would try them out very simply before getting into difficult drawing.

Talking about *The Thief and the Cobbler: A Moment in Time* at the screening at BFI Southbank – 25/11/2018 and 25/11/2018

We were breaking new ground in animation. We still are.

I actually really enjoyed seeing the film and noticed things I hadn't seen before.

Studying great films – 08/12/2018

I study silent movies – Chaplin, Keaton, Langdon, plus the great Russian silents. Plus Kurosawa. Especially Kurosawa.

On *A Christmas Carol* – 09/12/2018

We tried hard. The original Dickens story reads like a film script including special effects.

Off to London to BFI Southbank for a screening of a beautiful Academy restoration 35 mm print of *A Christmas Carol*. I got my first Oscar for this and I think it was the first Oscar for British animation. We couldn't have made it without the great animator Ken Harris and the work of Roy Naisbitt and Richard Purdum. There were the amazing voices of Alastair

Sim, Michael Hordern and Sir Michael Redgrave. The great Chuck Jones got us the job and last-minute help. It was made in seven months. Sleep was rationed. It was scary.

The book is systematic – 03/01/2019
The book is very systematic. I suggest copying a couple of walks at the same time you're trying on your own. That way you get the experience of our predecessors. Keep going.

On *The Animator's Survival Kit* when someone says – every animator should have a copy of this book – 12/02/2019
I have one. And I use it.

The iPad app – 12/02/2019
We worked really hard for a year to get the design right and the animated examples just as we wanted them. No sound on them – they're there for animation not entertainment.

Mistakes – 01/03/2019
We learn by doing and we learn by making mistakes. Animate as much as you can. Also copy walks from the book. Walks are the best way to learn.

3D animation – 17/03/2019
I think it's interesting, as is 2D animation. It's all very interesting.

Testing the information – 26/03/2019
That's great the book is a real help. The best thing is to test the information. Whenever I learned something I tested it to make sure it worked.

Keys – 06/04/2019
Keys are the storytelling drawings in the scene and extremes are the drawings where you get a change of direction. In a normal scene there are three or four storytelling positions but lots of extremes. I try to make this very clear in my book and iPad app.

Not a language of tongue – 06/04/2019
Animation is not a language of tongue. The knowledge is pictorial.

On the book and being lucky – 16/04/2019
Thank you, Jan. I'm glad you're finding it useful. I learned all this from the best of the best. I was very lucky.

The solution to a problem and taking one thing at a time – 11/04/2019 and
11/04/2019 and 19/04/2019
Today I have to take seven drawings, cut them out and stick 'em down in different positions. I'm doing a complicated turning zoom while a character gestures with a big hand up close. You can't rely on formulas, these things I am doing are challenging one-offs. Every one a battle.

The solution to my problem this morning is the usual one: remember to take one thing at a time.

To confirm what I said earlier about taking one thing at a time – I'm now able to resolve a really difficult problem by taking just one thing at a time. It's working well now.

My younger self – 13/05/2019
Surprised to see my younger self explaining animation on Bob Godfrey's BBC show in 1974. That's forty-five years ago! I don't disagree with what I'm saying. The basic thing is correct but there's a lot more to it if we want to sharpen.

On the Spanish edition – 27/05/2019
Because the book has been translated into so many languages I'd hoped it would also be translated into Spanish, because I know there are many talented Spanish and Latin American animators. I also lived in Spain for two years so: Arriba! Finally a Spanish edition has arrived and it looks great.

On *The Animator's Survival Kit* – 27/05/2019
I'm so happy it's useful. I sometimes go to it myself to refresh myself on something. It has so much information from so many clever people.

On what is going on today – 06/06/2019
You can do virtually anything today. The question is, what are you going to do that's generated by your talent? In my 2D world it started with drawing and I found the medium was capable of anything if I worked at it. I had what I needed.

On life drawing – 29/06/2019
We can never do enough life drawing. That includes me.

ACKNOWLEDGEMENTS

When Dick died, I wasn't sure whether I could or even should carry on with this book. My children Natasha and Leif Sutton-Williams waited patiently for me to decide. Once I'd made the decision that I was going to go ahead, they gave me endless encouragement and support. I couldn't have done it without their trust in me.

Our editor, Walter Donohue, also waited patiently for me to work out what I wanted to do. It turned out his patience needed to be endless – because this wasn't an easy journey. It was inevitably emotional going through Dick's history and our history together via old photos, drawings, paintings, notes, letters, transcripts, films and, above all, memories. It was early days to be trawling through our combined past and it had a cost. Sometimes I stopped to wonder if I was doing the right thing. But when I did, I rang Walter. I never had to tell him I was having doubts, I'd just discuss a specific issue or two. We'd chat around the problem, come up with a solution, and miraculously I'd be back working.

Walter has an amazing gift as an editor – he doesn't tell you what you should be doing, he finds out what you want to do and then helps you find a way to do it. He's done that for Dick and me for twenty-five years and neither of us could have completed the work we've done with Faber without him.

There are a number of institutions where we were lucky enough to meet incredible individuals who have supported our work: Randy Haberkamp at the Academy of Motion Picture Arts and Sciences, whose backing was crucial to saving *The Thief and the Cobbler* both as a film and as artwork, and who has supported us in every venture since we first met; Justin Johnson at the BFI Southbank, who arranged and moderated events with enthusiasm and energy over the years; Dave Kehr at MoMA, who screened *The Thief and the Cobbler: A Moment in Time* over several evenings; Howard Green from Disney, who arranged many LA dinners for us with the 'golden age' animators whom Dick admired so much, and who has always been there for us when we needed help; and Marcel Jean, the current Artistic Director of the Annecy International Animation Film Festival, who has sustained the warm friendship Dick had with the festival from its early days in 1958 to the masterclass we held in 2000 and the screening of our films over the years. Marcel has continued the tradition and always found a way to include us.

Dick, I know, would have wanted to reiterate his love and respect for the 'old guys' who transformed his adventures in animation with their knowledge, teaching and friendship. They include Dick Huemer, Ken Harris, Art Babbitt, Grim Natwick, Emery Hawkins and Milt Kahl (all of whom feature in this book), and also Ward Kimball, Frank Thomas and Ollie Johnston.

I'd like to thank members of Dick's family who dug deep into files and drawers to provide photos, letters and documents – his brother Tony Williams and sister-in-law Nancy Williams, his cousin Alan Bell and his eldest son Alex Williams. To my Dorset family – Philip Sutton, Saskia Sutton, Rebekah Sutton and Nick Beeks-Sanders – thank you for the dog walks by the sea, bottomless cups of tea and endless conversation. Much of the work on this book was done in various Dorset locations.

I'd like to thank John Cary for providing hitherto unknown cartoon drawings Dick made of himself and Tristram Cary while they worked together on *The Little Island*; Jane Willis – who has given advice and encouragement so generously over the years; Will Clarke for his friendship and professional back-up whenever it has been asked for; Frank Herrmann for the photos of Dick as a young man; Brian Harris for his photographs of our Camden studio at work; and Jaz Allen-Sutton for the photos of Dick in his basement studio.

John Canemaker was a friend of Dick's for over fifty years. They shared a passion for animation history and swapped stories and information, but more than that – they shared respect and admiration for each other's work. John has been infinitely helpful and a loyal supporter of this book right the way through.

The last ten years of Dick's working life were spent at Aardman. He described them as his happiest. He loved the community of working at the studio and made friends with and was supported by everyone there. So, thanks to Jo Johnson and the reception team for greeting him every day with delight; to the canteen team under Stuart Briggs for all the hot chocolate that sustained him; to Andy Janes who kept an eye on Dick out of his window and was there to help in any way he could; and above all to Peter Lord and David Sproxton, who thought we were staying a few months and put up with us for over ten years.

Aardman was the perfect working environment for Dick. *Prologue*, his last completed film, was finished there with the help of the compositing team led by Bram Ttwheam. So many people at Aardman made Dick's working life a joy, and my thanks go to you all.

Friends have sustained me in so many different ways and I couldn't have kept going without them: Angela and Martin Smith, Mario Jerome, John Hockey, Vanessa and Allan Ahlberg, Ellen Garvie, Karen Lord, Sue Giles, David Lloyd, David Robinson, Rob Coleman, Louise and Richard Walker, Mags and Nick Park, Alan Snow, Ben Smith, Jane Taube and Carole Jones, Su-Min and Grace Lee, Val Thomas and Samia Al Qadhi.

Dick and I have worked on various projects with Faber since 1997. The team I've worked with over the past few years – including freelancers – has been particularly generous and sensitive to my unusual situation. So, huge thanks to: Pedro Nelson, Lizzie Bishop, Mallory Ladd, Sophie Clarke, Arabella Watkiss, Paddy Fox, Ray Goodey, Amanda Russell, Kate Hopkins and Sarah Barlow.

There is someone I have to credit with keeping the whole thing together and improving the book at every stage of its production. It has not been a simple task. Kate Ward, the Editorial Design Manager at Faber, has been an absolute marvel throughout. She has encouraged, guided, gently nudged in the right direction, and has always gone well beyond the call of duty, while keeping me involved in every stage of the process. I'm endlessly grateful.

The final acknowledgement has to go to Dick. This book was created first alongside and then without my husband of thirty-five years. It is written both with him and for him. Our last collaboration.

Imogen Sutton, 2024

IMAGE CREDITS

All images are from the collection of Richard Williams except for the following:

Every effort has been made to trace or contact all copyright holders. The publishers would be pleased to rectify at the earliest opportunity any omissions or errors brought to their notice.